Church at the Crossroads

Michael Marshall

Church at the Crossroads

Lambeth 1988

St. Mark's Church
Highland, MD 20777

1817

Harper & Row, Publishers, San Francisco
Cambridge, Hagerstown, New York, Philadelphia, Washington
London, Mexico City, São Paulo, Singapore, Sydney

Collins Liturgical Publications
8 Grafton Street, London W1X 3LA

Harper & Row, San Francisco
Icehouse One — 401
151 Union Street, San Francisco, CA 94111–1299

Collins Liturgical in Canada
Novalis, Box 9700, Terminal,
375 Rideau St, Ottawa, Ontario K1G 4B4

Collins Dove
PO Box 316, Blackburn, Victoria 3130

Collins Liturgical New Zealand
PO Box 1, Auckland

Page 6 and the picture of Archbishop Longley on p. 10: by permission of the Archbishop of Canterbury; copyright reserved to the Church Commissioners and Courtauld Institute of Arts

Page 10: The Lambeth Conference in 1867, by permission of U.S.P.G.

Page 107: by permission of U.S.P.G.

Cover design by Leigh Hurlock
Typographical design by Malcolm Harvey Young
Typeset by Swains (Glasgow) Ltd

FIRST EDITION

Library of Congress Catalog Number: 88-45732

ISBN: 0-06-065427-9

88 89 90 91 92 HC 10 9 8 7 6 5 4 3 2 1

To Stephen Bayne
an heroic architect of Anglicanism

'There is such a thing as Anglican theology and it is sorely needed at the present day. But because it is neither a system nor a confession . . . but a method, a use and a direction, it cannot be defined or even perceived as a "thing in itself", and it may elude the eyes of those who ask "What is it?" and "Where is it?". It has been proved, and will be proved again, by its fruits and its works.'
Bishop Michael Ramsey

Contents

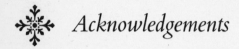

Acknowledgements

The author wishes to express his gratitude to many people who have made this book possible. *The Anglican Digest* and the Episcopal Book Club have vigorously supported the project from the outset by making funds available for the extensive travelling involved in researching this book as well as by paying for my expenses during the Lambeth Conference and in the busy days afterwards for the completion of the manuscript.

The Anglican Institute made time available in my hectic schedule for several visits to England and also provided me with the good services of Sally Barrett, my Personal Assistant, who has extensively researched this book and seen it through its many stages.

Necessarily for a book to be produced so swiftly it has required a team of people, ready and willing to burn the midnight oil. Georgia Streett, my colleague and Associate Director of The Anglican Institute has given wings to every resource of modern technology to make sure that the right number of words was in the right place at the right time.

Sally Ferard of Collins went well beyond the call of duty to ensure the manuscripts were well edited and that we stayed on target with a tight time-schedule for publication. Bob Byers, the Communications Officer for the Anglican Consultative Council and his secretary, cooperated at every stage by their availability and guidance.

My gratitude also is called for and readily expressed to Canon Sam Van Culin, the Secretary-General at the Anglican Consultative Council, for writing the foreword to the book and for his generous friendship and support over the four years I have spent at The Anglican Institute in the United States of America. Jonathan Prichard kindly researched the photographs for the book.

Foreword ❋

We need our stories. We need to narrate as well as to listen. Our stories help to define who we are and, as our theologians have reminded us, that our stories can be expressions of theological insight.

The Lambeth Conference of '88 has its story. When the Archbishop of Canterbury asked the bishops to bring their diocese with them, he was, in effect, inviting them to come to the Conference prepared to tell their story. Many bishops have done so, movingly, haltingly, anxiously, but always in the understanding that each story, however apparently dramatic or insignificant, is part of the filaments of our common life.

The filaments are spun wider even than this. For Lambeth '88 is not just made up of its own stories; it is itself, as the twelfth in a succession of Lambeth Conferences, part of a larger and longer story that stretches back to Archbishop Longley and the first Lambeth Conference in 1867. And more recently the Anglican story has deepened and broadened as new Provinces have taken root in their own soils and as the Anglican Consultative Council has developed, and the Primates' Meetings have become a regular feature of our common life.

Michael Marshall sets his account of Lambeth '88 in the context of some of this greater Anglican story, and I commend the attempt. We must be grounded in our Anglican story. We shall then be the more able to do the work that, as individual churches, we are called to do in the different places where God summons us to live out our own stories.

'Our unity', to quote Stephen Bayne, to whom this book is fittingly dedicated, 'lies not in our thinking alike, but in our acting together.' Nothing could better describe the Lambeth Conference; and perhaps nothing could better describe our story as the Anglican Communion.

Samuel Van Culin   COMPASROSE
Secretary, Lambeth Conference 1988 London

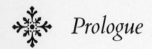 *Prologue*

The story of ecclesiastical councils and synodical gatherings is not a very happy record from the files of Church history. They do not make for very edifying reading. Usually they have not had a good press. Furthermore, with the built-in advantage of hindsight, armchair critics swiftly emerge from the woodwork, impatient to point out the failings and errors of such deliberations, confident that all such gatherings are doomed to failure at worst, and at best only achieve the mediocrity of platitudes and face-saving resolutions.

Moreover, although bishops are given to chorusing enthusiastically about collegiality, they are somewhat better at singing about it than engaging in it. This should not be a cause for surprise. As a personality type, bishops are frequently drawn from that group of people who are used to being the largest fish in their particular pond — which they delight to call their jurisdiction. Add to this the particular chemistry of Anglicanism, which somewhat like the weather begs comment and opinion from every uninformed quarter, and it is not difficult to see why the prospect of another Lambeth Conference might well be explosive at best or a damp squib at worst.

Before Lambeth '88 Jonahs and Jeremiahs alike had spoken of the end of the Anglican Communion, the last of the Lambeth Conferences, and of Dr Runcie's 'fragmented flock'. Ecclesiastical forecasters had no difficulty in foreseeing the approach of storms, crises and divisions at Lambeth '88. Everyone from the Archbishop of Canterbury to Dr Spong of Newark, USA, had clearly foreseen that the issues of unity and authority might not bode well for a successful or a fruitful Lambeth Conference. By the time 17th July dawned — the first day of the Conference — observers and reporters crowded around Canterbury with a mixture of that embarrassment and expectation experienced by parents while waiting for the curtain to go up on the end-of-term school play or concert. Should we applaud, smile, condescend, criticize, or write it off as not even worthy of our attention?

To tell the truth, Lambeth '88 surprised itself. In fact, it will almost certainly be seen as an occasion when the place of Anglicanism in the worldwide Church was stoutly reaffirmed. For in practice it was the crisis which occasioned new commitment and the crossroads which facilitated convergence and meeting. In an age of compulsive certainties, Anglicanism may yet emerge with the ability to recall humanity to the way of faith, discipleship and pilgrimage. 'We walk by faith and not by sight', should be the text from St Paul to all who are committed to exploration and adventure.

For crisis and commitment can hang together: crossroads really are for meeting. It was G.K. Chesterton, that craggy pilgrim who delighted in paradox, who said that the cross as the sign of Christianity was purposefully the very opposite of the sign of all other religions, a circle. For the cross stands like a signpost at the place where apparently opposing truths meet in the collision of paradox, and from which travellers and pilgrims are sent out to the four corners of the earth. In contrast, there is something excluding and exclusive about the circle: it needs to be broken open by apparent conflict and contradiction if it is not to become claustrophobic and ingrown.

The bishops could have left Lambeth, neatly in step, having attained the wrong kind of unity and proclaiming a very un-Christian kind of authority. 'The world is used to unity of all sorts,' warned Elizabeth Templeton during the first week of Lambeth,

'to the unity of solidarity in campaigns, unity in resistance, communities of party, creed, interest. But it is not used to such possibilities as this: that, for example, those who find the exclusion of women from the priesthood an intolerable apartheid and those who find the inclusion a violation of God's will should enter upon one another's suffering. Somewhere in there, authority lies.'

With the benefit of hindsight we shall probably realize that we only find the signposts at the crossroads — at the place where the roads leading in different directions converge. We discover our commitment in and at the very point of crisis, and we discover that, after all, the crisis was the catalyst which leads to a new ferment of deeper fellowship, lasting loyalties and true community. Armchair critics, who prefer the security of staying at home, will naturally call for clear and infallible maps from such meetings as Lambeth, maps with dogmatic and unquestionable statements, ready to be catalogued and promptly shelved. Pilgrims and travellers, all ready for the unexpected, are content with signposts – which are neither more nor less than they claim to be: legible directions pointing beyond themselves to new horizons and unexplored lands.

'I suspect that only from such depths of exploration which Churches rarely expose themselves to, will unity or authority emerge, at least in any sense which makes us credible as agents of God's healing in a broken world.' (Elizabeth Templeton)

If that is the kind of unity and authority we sought at Lambeth '88, history may show that we discovered more there than we ever realized. This book will infuriate the pathological critic of Anglicanism. Hopefully it might stimulate or even encourage the enquirer, the disciple, or the committed Anglican who has lost some nerve in recent years. Anglicanism, like democracy, tends not to have much going for it until you begin to contemplate the alternatives. Lambeth '88 refused to 'hare' after any of those strangely seductive alternatives. In that it achieved this, it should be commended and even modestly applauded.

✠Michael Marshall
6th August, 1988

Stop Press Acknowledgements

This book makes no attempt to satisfy the research of serious scholars. Such needs will only be met by the formal report, the detailed resolutions and the Pastoral Letters, all of which will be published later in 1988. This was a swift publication, off the cuff of a pilgrim who was privileged to be present at Lambeth '88. In order to achieve the deadline for publication the author is profoundly indebted to several people whose names should be acknowledged with gratitude in this book.

Stephen Webb, John Miles, Charles Long and Ben May, the official photographer to Lambeth, have all contributed to the selection of photgraphs. Thanks must go too to the Revd Giles Harcourt. The Communications Team during Lambeth was generous with time and help during their extremely exacting programme, especially Flavia Gonsalves. Much gratitude is owed to the many different participants in the Conference who gave of their time to be interviewed for contributions to this book.

Church at the Crossroads

PART ONE

An Evolving Church

CHAPTER ONE

Glimpses of Lambeth Conferences through the Years (1867–1978)

'It must be remembered that it is a serious matter to gather the Bishops together from all parts of the globe, unless there is some distinct object for their so gathering. I therefore am disposed, by the advice of my brethren, to request that our brethren at home, and also those at a distance, will state to me as explicitly as possible what the objects are that it is desirable to discuss at such a meeting. They are of a somewhat limited character.'[1]

Archbishop Tait

Getting them all together

'It cannot be', said Archbishop Cosmo Gordon Lang in Canterbury Cathedral, at the opening service of the seventh Lambeth Conference in 1930: 'It cannot be that He means us to come and go and leave nothing but a string of platitudes behind us.'[2] Hopefully not, yet perhaps the time is ripe to look back over the last hundred and twenty years or so, and over the formidable piles of paper, the hours of speeches, and the reports and resolutions which have issued from a dozen such Lambeth Conferences to see if, when the dust has settled, there is anything more visible and evident left behind than 'a string of platitudes'.

Archbishop Lang, perhaps one of the more aristocratic archbishops in recent decades, had stood by the Chair of St Augustine to receive over three hundred and fifty bishops and delegates. 'It was indeed moving to see this great company of Bishops from every part of the world,' he recalled, 'slowly and with ordered dignity passing before me as I stood at that Chair.'[3] So the seventh Lambeth Conference began. 'To me,' said Lang, 'the most moving part of the service

1

was the singing, strong, full, exultant, of Heber's hymn, "Holy, Holy, Holy, Lord God Almighty", immediately after the Creed.'[4] Lang had been somewhat apprehensive about the Lambeth Conference in 1930. In the weeks leading up to the Conference, at the age of sixty-six, he had not enjoyed the best of health, and the prospect of extending hospitality to over three hundred bishops, at Lambeth Palace, on the slender resources afforded to him by special grants from the Church Assembly was understandably somewhat chilling and daunting. For over a period of five weeks all the bishops had to be entertained to luncheon and tea each day, while bishops from overseas (together with their wives) would be invited to spend one night within the walls of the Tudor palace of Lambeth — perhaps, on the principle of osmosis, to catch something from the ghost of Cranmer and the spirit of Anglicanism.

Each and every evening there would have been a party to receive not only the bishops but delegates from other Churches such as the Orthodox Churches and Old Catholic Churches. For hospitality, like worship, is an essential ingredient in an environment of collegiality: talking and conferring should surely for Christians be set in the wider context of worship and fellowship engendered within the household of faith. This dimension has proved more and not less important as successive Lambeth Conferences have gone by. Hence the decision to hold (for the first time) the Lambeth Conference of 1978 in the residential setting of the University of Kent just outside Canterbury — a safe distance perhaps from the distractions offered by the lights of London, the theatres and luxurious clerical outfitters. Latter day Lambeth Conferences have given extended space to the participants for meditation, prayer and worship and Lambeth '88 was no exception.

The lengthy preface to the eighty-fifth edition of *Crockford's Clerical Directory* in 1975 had called for a new emphasis upon prayer and reflection in subsequent Lambeth Conferences and hoped that the next Lambeth would be

> 'regarded primarily as an opportunity for prayer, reflection, and training, rather than as a factory of the turgidly generalized, so-called "resolutions" to which international conferences are all too prone.'[5]

Lang had begun the Lambeth Conference in 1930 with a devotional day held at Fulham Palace for all the bishops. The address was given by the old and venerable Bishop Talbot, aged eighty-six. He had recently fallen and broken his thigh. His son (the Bishop of Pretoria) practically carried his old father. Bishop Talbot was the last remaining link with the great days of the Oxford Movement — a nineteenth century renewal movement which had begun in the 1830's. We are told that the 'mere sight of the old man, with his rugged head and beard and clear voice was more moving than any words.'[6] For what is certain is that every Lambeth Conference will indeed be a factory of words and more words. Yet, it may not be too much to say, that for many the addresses given by Metropolitan Anthony Bloom at the opening of the 1978 Lambeth Conference were among the highlights of the Conference of that year. For the collegial mentality and atmosphere afforded by this kind of hospitality and reflection on a university campus have never been possible either at Lambeth Palace or Church House, Westminster (the setting for the heavily paper-weighted Lambeth of 1968). The concentration afforded by residential Lambeth Conferences ('78 and '88) has helped in no small way to give the sense of belonging to a worldwide family. 'Worshipping and praying day by day as one body,' wrote Bishop Howe of the experience of the '78 Conference,

> 'was made possible as never before. Because it was an expression of Anglican universalism as it is, there was appreciation of the use of rites, and sometimes languages, that were unfamiliar to many, but all of which derived from current practice in the Anglican Communion . . . It was features like these in the Conference of 1978 that accounted for one Archbishop, from Africa, observing that "for me the Anglican Communion has come alive for the first time, and it feels like home"; and an English Archbishop saying, "I felt I was at the re-birth of the Anglican Communion — a kind of recapitulation with a long evolution ahead."'[7]

Establishing a tradition

For truth to tell, the 1978 Conference was a long road ahead of all the well-intentioned arrangements of Archbishop Lang in 1930 and certainly of Archbishop Longley in the dark ages of the very first, tentative Lambeth Conference of 1867. Of course at that first Lambeth

Conference there had only been a handful of bishops present — some seventy-six in number. (The Archbishop of York and the Bishops of Durham, Peterborough and Manchester, among others, had chosen to absent themselves.)

'Your Grace', beseeched the tenacious Bishop Lewis of Canada in 1866 in approaching Archbishop Longley about a possible Lambeth gathering of some sort: 'Do we not all belong to the same family? Why should we not meet?'[8] And so they did and so they do. It was, in fact, the persistence of the Province of Canada which can take credit for finally persuading the reluctant Archbishop Longley to undertake such an enterprise. The bishops, clergy and laity of that far-flung province set forth clearly the reasons for calling together such a conference.

> 'In order, therefore, to comfort the souls of the faithful, and reassure the minds of wavering members of the Church, and to obviate, as far as may be, the suspicion whereby so many are scandalized, that the Church is a creation of Parliament, we humbly entreat your Grace, since the assembling of a General Council of the whole Catholic Church is at present impracticable, to convene a National Synod of the Bishops of the Anglican Church at home and abroad, who, attended by one or more of their presbyters or laymen, learned in ecclesiastical law, as their advisers, may meet together, and, under the guidance of the Holy Ghost, take counsel and adopt such measures, as may be best fitted to provide for the present distress, in such a Synod, presided over by your Grace.'[9]

The Province of Canada was not alone in discerning the need for some kind of Anglican gathering, convened under the chairmanship of the Archbishop of Canterbury. Anglican affairs both in England for the Church of England, as well as in provinces further afield like South Africa, were proving to be stormy and potentially divisive in the 1860's. Later on in the 1860's some leading churchmen published a book of essays under the collective title, *Essays and Reviews*. In a word, this volume made 'popular' (though surely in a relative sense) the early and radical findings of biblical criticism. The Church of England, perhaps for the first time since the Reformation, was called upon to declare what it believed and how it arrived at such beliefs. It has to be said that the same challenge faces the bishops at Lambeth Conferences to this day. In many ways all subsequent Lambeth Conferences have revolved around a similar theme with only slightly differing variations.

For if Anglicanism prides itself on comprehensiveness, the question still needs to be put: how comprehensive is comprehensive? Or put another way, when is an Anglican not an Anglican? Since the beginnings of the nineteenth century it is the beliefs as well as the practices of Anglicanism which have become increasingly divisive. The only difference between the theological backdrop to the first Conference of 1867 and the Lambeth Conference of 1988 is the scale of division and disagreement: the theological gnats which irritated Archbishop Longley in the 1860's have grown into a stampede of elephants for Archbishop Runcie and the Lambeth Fathers of the 1988 Lambeth Conference. The biblical criticism contained within *Essays and Reviews* strikes but a few notes on the piccolo of heterodoxy in the nineteenth century compared with the Wagnerian score of grievances of the 1980's. Today, in some areas of Anglicanism the scriptures are not merely critically studied but virtually written off as culturally conditioned and as almost totally irrelevant to any discussions on matters so widely ranging and diverse as homosexual life-style, women bishops and inclusive God language. 'Present distress' was in the air at that first Lambeth Conference and has remained, at least in the background, at all subsequent Lambeth gatherings.

We need to note that in that first request from Canada for some kind of pan-Anglican gathering, there was no doubt in the minds of the supplicants that such a gathering should be presided over by his Grace, the Archbishop of Canterbury, successor to St Augustine of Canterbury, and Primate of all England. It was not for nothing that Archbishop Lang seized theatrical advantage by receiving all the bishops at the 1930 Conference 'standing by the Chair of Augustine'. The imagery is compelling and the symbolism is authentic and powerful.

Nurturing Lambeth Conferences

Each successive Archbishop of Canterbury has to some greater or lesser extent put something of the seal of his own personality upon Lambeth Conferences.

Necessarily, however, the role of the Archbishop of Canterbury

... that seat of St Augustine: some notable Archbishops

Archbishop Tait
Chairman 1878
Lambeth Conference

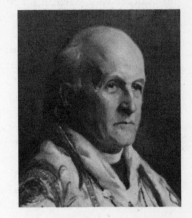

Archbishop Lang
Chairman 1930
Lambeth Conference

Archbishop Fisher
Chairman 1948 and 1958
Lambeth Conferences

Archbishop Ramsey
Chairman 1968
Lambeth Conference

and his relationship to Lambeth Conferences has always been a subtle and sensitive one. For leadership and direction, the assembled Bishops instinctively turn to the incumbent of that seat of St Augustine. Yet it is not by right nor by any written constitution that Archbishops of Canterbury have played this role. It was in fact an American Bishop — the Bishop of Iowa — who wrote with such warmth and praise of Archbishop Tait's chairmanship of the second Lambeth Conference in 1878.

'As the host of a hundred Bishops who recognize in him, if not a patriarchal dignity, a pre-eminence willingly and reverently accorded to the incumbent of the chair of St Augustine of Canterbury . . . While avoiding all appearance of dictation, his presence and position were always felt; and the harmony and unanimity of the Conference were largely due to his uniform affability and good temper and his masterly leadership.'[10]

Similar praise was afforded to Archbishop Fisher, especially at his first Lambeth Conference as chairman in 1948, and again from the Church in the United States. Bishop Sherrill said quite simply that

'the arrangements were perfect. Both the Archbishop and Mrs Fisher were so hospitable. They entertained scores of Bishops and their wives, both at Lambeth and at the Old Palace in Canterbury. This was especially difficult in 1948, when there were such great shortages both of food and of help. They showed a great concern for the comfort of all. All this resulted in the happiest atmosphere throughout the Conference and had a great effect upon the discussions . . . I cannot recall hearing an unhappy or critical remark by any of our Bishops or their wives — no small achievement in itself . . . It was the Archbishop's own personality which made the new spirit within the Anglican Communion. At a critical period of change and re-adjustment, he made a contribution which has made possible future growth and development.'[11]

It was said that Fisher ruled the English House of Bishops like a headmaster with his school prefects and in many ways the same applied, *a fortiori,* to his handling of the two Lambeth Conferences of 1948 and 1958. Indeed, at the end of the final session of his second Lambeth Conference in 1958, he concluded with the authoritative words: 'Class dismissed!'

In fact, Fisher had been uniquely and powerfully moved at the end of the final service in Westminster Abbey after the Conference in 1958. Over many years, both he and Mrs Fisher had built up strong ties of friendship in the Anglican Communion, and perhaps this is the secret of the unity of a living communion: the head, whose only qualification for such a title is his readiness to be, in some sense, 'servant of all'. There has to be a strong *philadelphia* (love of the brotherhood) which binds all together in unity and fellowship, and which is stronger than any one issue or cause however powerfully championed by individual members of the Body.

'Never in my life,' recalled Fisher,

'have I been so moved as at the closing service in Westminster Abbey at the end of the Conference (1958), when Henry Sherrill preached the sermon, and we went in procession from the Abbey to the Chapter House, all the Bishops of the Anglican Communion. There I bade them farewell. There immediately in front of me was Owen, Archbishop of New Zealand, who had been up at Oxford with me, and then headmaster at Uppingham when I was headmaster at Repton. There were all the others. I knew that I should never see Owen or many of them again. I did just say a few words of farewell to them all, a word of gratitude and love and affection, and had to turn away as they ended, because I could not trust myself to say more.'[12]

Yes, there perhaps is the secret of it all. After the Second World War, it had been a long time since the Bishops had met at Lambeth (1930). It was clearly time to bring them all together again.

'One problem loomed at the outset. The question was whether the Bishops would come, because travel was expensive, and it was a great business to leave their dioceses, often shattered by war experience.'[13]

There were other difficulties. 'It was no secret,' Fisher said,

'but many of the bishops of the Church in the United States, as well as others in the Anglican Communion outside England, had not felt happy about their place in the Lambeth Conference of 1930. They had felt in essence that they were onlookers rather than participants. In fact, some of our Bishops said that they would not attend another Conference.'[14]

So Archbishop Fisher began, on a largely unprecedented scale, to become the travelling ambassador in the name of Anglicanism. His successors have taken up this role ever since – none more so, let it be said, than the present incumbent of the See of Canterbury. ('The Archbishop,' (Runcie), says one writer, 'is filled, obsessed one might say, with a sense of the international significance of the Anglican Church.'[15])

To help in all of this, Fisher appointed Bishop Stephen Bayne as the first Executive Officer of Anglicanism (see page 16). His travels became legendary and, in their turn, his successors in that role have travelled extensively throughout the Communion, building up bonds of friendship which have proved invaluable in securing truly representative gatherings at Lambeth. It has become increasingly clear that the successor to St Augustine (himself something of a traveller and ambassador) needs to take seriously this aspect of his work, and that this dimension of an Archbishop of Canterbury's workload is likely to increase rather than decrease with the course of time. The pay-off in Lambeth '88 of travelling-time spent by Archbishop Runcie visiting the far-flung parts of the Anglican Churches is hard to over-estimate.

But what sort of Conference?

But to go back to the beginning. Archbishop Longley, aged seventy-three at the first Lambeth Conference, was tentative in acceding to the request of the Province of Canada and saw his job primarily in terms of cooling off any passionate debate, calming controversy and getting everybody home and back to work with the minimum of debate or discussion. He had sent out the invitations to the bishops as late as the end of February, although the Conference, which was to last for only four days, was due to begin in September of the same year. He had been a hard-working bishop for thirty years, but he was 'scarcely a constructive ecclesiastical statesman'.[16] Indeed it is perhaps not too much to say that the 'most memorable event of his rather undistinguished Archiepiscopate was'[17] that first Lambeth Conference. Longley was aware that such a conference was (to use his own words) 'entirely without precedent.' Not unnaturally, there was no lack of opposition for such an unprecedented gathering.

The First Lambeth Conference, 1867

Archbishop Longley

The bishops in front of Lambeth Palace

From the outset, from the point of view of many, it was in the first place the wrong sort of conference. There were those who, like Bishop Selwyn of New Zealand, attended the first Lambeth Conference with great eagerness yet who would have much preferred a kind of pan-Anglican synodical gathering. 'Synodical action is so familiar to me that I can neither share the fears of the Bishop of St David's,' he wrote, 'nor care for the sneers of the Dean of Westminster.'[18]

After all, we need to recall at least with some imagination the limited and rather tunnel-vision of Church leaders in the Church of England in the mid-nineteenth century. Tied constitutionally and firmly to the apron-strings of Parliament, and with all major appointments still in the hands of the Monarch, advised by the Prime Minister, the Church of England had no reason to seek participation in strange and unconstitutional conferences — and certainly not if they involved making any real and substantial decisions in matters of doctrine or ecclesiastical order. This was the era of Queen Victoria, who liked her clergymen to be broad churchmen of the liberal persuasion. She approved neither of Evangelicals nor of Tractarians.

'When Davidson became her adviser he was formally instructed that neither of these categories were to be promoted. She wanted moderate churchmen. "It is by such appointments alone," she told Disraeli in 1874, "that we can hope to strengthen the very tottering fabric of the Established Church. The extreme Evangelical school do the Established Church as much harm as the High Church."'[19]

Fortunately, thanks to Disraeli, Gladstone and Salisbury, Victoria did not always get her own way about ecclesiastical appointments.

'She was oddly suspicious of clergymen who tried to do good to the poor. When the Dean of Windsor visited one of her coachmen in his illness, she did not quite like it. She advised Davidson not to visit too much.'[20]

What should they talk about?

All this characterized a well-intentioned environment prevalent in the Church of England, yet one seriously limited by the tunnel-vision of Victorian imperialism. However it was this same environment, with all its limitations, out of which Lambeth Conferences in particular and the Anglican Communion in general were born. Furthermore, it was the environment into which Longley, Tait, Davidson and Benson invited zealots and missionaries from overseas for the purpose of deliberation. That the Lambeth Conferences achieved perhaps rather little is not a cause for scorn; that they have achieved anything at all should be cause for thanksgiving. Archbishop Longley was quite adamant from the outset: 'Such a meeting would not be competent to make declarations, or lay down definitions on points of doctrine.'

Archbishop Tait was equally clear in his mind about the limitations that should be set upon the agenda and expectations of Lambeth Conferences, which he regarded as the 'most delicate and complicated of the Primate's manifold responsibilities'.[21]

He was well aware that his predecessor [Longley] 'had a very difficult task in defining the exact duty of the Bishops who came together on the former occasion. And with great firmness, and at the same time with that remarkable courtesy and kindliness for which he was so eminent, he steered the somewhat difficult course'[22] of saying (some would rather cynically comment) absolutely nothing whatever of any significance.

That is not true. Throughout the years, Lambeth Conferences have explored the mind of the Bishops on matters ranging from birth control (1930) to the nature of authority in Anglicanism in an especially masterly statement (1948). In 1920 (perhaps one of the better organized Lambeth Conferences) the Lambeth Fathers had spoken with power and authority on matters of war and peace in a Europe which was only just recovering from the slaughter of the First World War. In many cases, Lambeth Conferences have issued helpful guidelines and have addressed the issues of their day as well as the more domestic concerns of ecclesiastical life.

Yet from the beginning it has been perfectly clear: Lambeth Conferences have no juridical power to bind or loose any or all of the constituent Churches on matters of doctrine or church order. Lambeth Conferences from the outset have been and remain purely consultative, while speaking with considerable authority and drawing upon widely diverse experiences and insights.

So it was that Archbishop Tait followed the precedent, set without precedent, by Charles Longley in the first Conference when he summoned the second Lambeth Conference in 1878 (see also page 35ff). Significantly, it was the American House of Bishops who began to press Archbishop Tait for a second Lambeth Conference as early as 1874 — only seven years after the first Conference chaired so swiftly by Archbishop Longley. Tait was a Scotsman, the first Scottish Archbishop of Canterbury. He was cautious and not prepared to undertake another Lambeth gathering without the full support of the English bishops — notably and especially the bishops and archbishop of the Northern Province. Furthermore, he was quite clear in his mind that Longley had sailed somewhat close to the wind and had only just avoided a full-blown storm. If there was to be a second conference, it was too soon — ten years, he felt, should be the minimum gap between such conferences.

Furthermore, next time — if there was to be a next time (undoubtedly the most consistent question raised at every successive Lambeth Conference to the present day) 'there should be no misunderstanding' said Tait to his Convocation,

> 'and none of that difficulty, which, I am bound to say, did exist at the last Lambeth Conference, as to what subjects might and what subjects might not be introduced; that we should know what it is that our brethren wish to bring before us, and what we wish to bring before them, before they give themselves the trouble of coming from the ends of the earth.'[23]

One thing was clear to Tait — even more clear than it had been to Archbishop Longley.

> 'There is no intention whatever on the part of anybody to gather together the bishops of the Anglican Church for the sake of defining any matter of doctrine.'[24]

As it was in the beginning, is now and ever shall be — Anglicans, somewhat strong on meetings and discussion, but rather weak on doctrine!

However, after much consultation, and fortified by the concurrence of the Northern Convocation, Archbishop Tait sent out a letter on 28 March 1876 to all the bishops of the Anglican Communion soliciting their wishes concerning a possible second Lambeth Conference to be held in 1878.

'Before the close of the year about ninety letters of reply were received . . . an overwhelming preponderance of opinion in favour . . . provided a longer period of session could be arranged for than "the four short days" of 1867.'[25]

So Lambeth in its first decade, had, like topsy, grown from four days to four weeks! From seventy-six in attendance to exactly one hundred. Tradition was now established and there was no turning back. Even the phrase 'Anglican Communion' was here and here to stay — at least for the next hundred years. Yet Tait was too much the diplomatist and too much the evangelist and missionary to allow maintenance to displace mission or paper to overtake proclamation. 'Some people think there is a danger in the present day lest Churches should occupy themselves too much with minor matters,' he reminded the assembled bishops in his opening speech at the Conference. 'After all, it is the spread of the Eternal Gospel of Jesus Christ, that we all have at heart.'[26] And it was true: although with the advantage of retrospective assessment we can see that the Church of England was in decline by the close of the nineteenth century, it did not feel like that to Gladstone when he wrote to the Queen in 1874:

'For centuries there has not been a time of so much practical and hearty work, so much earnest preaching, so much affectionate care for the poor and for the young.'[27]

Re-establishing Lambeth Conferences after 1945

It was probably with Fisher at Canterbury in the Conferences of 1948 and 1958 that Lambeth Conferences reached their high watermark of confidence, attendance and sense of *esprit de corps*. After Fisher's celebrated sermon in 1946 when he appealed to the Free Churches to take episcopacy into their system and leading up to his famous visit to Jerusalem, Istanbul and finally to Rome itself and Pope John XXIII, there was an increasing confidence in ecumenism and the part that Anglicanism could play in it.

At that time, however, in matters ecumenical, the stumbling block in Lambeth Conferences proved to be the status of the Church of

South India and to this day its relations to the Anglican Communion have remained something of an anomaly. Nevertheless, after the ravages of World War II there was a genuine desire within all the Churches to mirror back to the nations of the world an image and an icon of reconciliation, that they would know that we were his disciples 'by our love'. This was to be seen in ecclesiastical terms not by 'takeover' bids or by subsuming parts of Churches into larger Churches, but rather by pressing forward to a unity and enrichment which drew upon valid and authentic traditions. Anglicanism by its very diversity clearly had a part to play in all this.

Again it was Fisher, that 'headmaster with an outreach',[28] as Carpenter describes him, who set the pace not only in his Cambridge sermon, but in his encounter with Pope John XXIII. At one point the Pope read in English a passage in which he expressed his deep desire that the time would soon come 'when our separated brethren should return to the Mother Church'. The Most Reverend headmaster could not resist the temptation to correct the Pope. 'Your Holiness, not *return?*' The Pope looked puzzled and said, 'Not return? Why not?' Fisher retorted: 'None of us can go backwards. We are each now running on parallel courses; we are looking forward, until, in God's time, our two courses approximate and meet.' The Pope, after a moment's pause, replied, 'You are right.'[29] That was indeed an historic moment when an infallible Pope told a fallible Archbishop and headmaster that he, rather than the Pope, was right! It proved, however, to be a new step along the road which was humbly and wonderfully pursued by Fisher's successor on his historic visit to Rome and finally in the visit of Pope John Paul to Canterbury and Archbishop Runcie in 1982.

The Conference of 1948 took up this theme of ecumenism with a passion, relating it directly to such themes as racial prejudice, discrimination, the torments and divisions of Palestine. It was also the 1948 Conference which received the report on the nature of unity and authority in the Anglican Communion (see page 74ff). In many ways that particular report (which was never a resolution) has weathered well and has, in fact, become the classical statement about authority in Anglicanism. It is one of the really superb pieces of work to emerge out of Lambeth deliberations.

Communication in a worldwide communion

It became increasingly clear after something of the euphoria of the post-war years and the unprecedented and genuine affection for Fisher in his long primacy building up to the 1958 Conference, that Lambeth Conferences needed to be much more carefully prepared if there was to be genuine participation from all the bishops. Some of the rumblings of the 1930 Conference were back again, and it became clear to Archbishop Ramsey that the 1968 Conference would have to be well prepared and must marshal the forces and abilities of as many bishops as possible throughout the world.

The 1958 Conference had spoken of the appointment of an Anglican Executive Officer and eventually Archbishop Fisher announced the appointment of Bishop Stephen F. Bayne, who was Bishop of Olympia in the United States and who took up the post from March 1959. The terms of his appointment were as non-constricting as possible and were worded in typical Fisher style.

'At the request of the Lambeth Conference, in 1958, the Metropolitans of the Anglican Communion have appointed a new officer with the title of Anglican Executive Officer. The chief duties are on the one hand to act as a controller of the Anglican Advisory Council on Missionary Strategy and on the other hand to exercise a general supervision on behalf of the Consultative Body of the Lambeth Conference on all matters affecting the Anglican Communion which call for attention between the decennial conferences.

As the office is a new one it will be for this first holder of it to discover how best to fulfil these duties and to render his best service to the various Provinces of the Anglican Communion in their joint concerns.'[30]

Note, now, the apparently accepted expectation that Lambeth Conferences would occur every ten years and furthermore that there would be continuous work of liaising and communicating in the years after and leading up to each Conference. The Lambeth Conferences would simply not have survived on the 'old-boy network'. They needed and will continue to need permanent servicing. It was to this end that Bishop Stephen Bayne brought all his ability, commitment and warm personality. 'The choice of Stephen Bayne was inspired', writes Alan Stephenson. 'He made an immense success of the new office, and soon became a well-known figure both in this country (England) and throughout the whole Anglican Communion, where he travelled very widely.'[31]

For 'his personality', wrote Roger Lloyd, 'was exactly suited to the task he had accepted. Pleasant and easy in manner, he was most likeable, and he had the gift of bestowing on all others the ease he had himself in all manner of conversation. There was depth and often profundity in his speeches and his writing.'[32] Here at last was the tangible link and personal servant for the wider communion of Churches, who would develop the life of Anglicanism through continuous conference and dialogue. The staccato and intermittent effect of decennial conferences would no longer work, and without the ministry of Stephen Bayne and his successors, John Howe and Sam Van Culin (under different appointment names) together with the Anglican Consultative Council of today, Anglicanism would have fragmented long ago. That is not an overstatement. The work of the ACC and its Secretary General must necessarily increase in importance and volume in the coming years while in no way detracting from the necessary and important personal role of the Archbishop of Canterbury as co-ordinator of the Primates and as the obvious President and Chairman of the Lambeth Conference gathering.

The 'new-style' Conference of 1968

Immediately, on the morning after his enthronement as Archbishop of Canterbury in June 1961, Archbishop Michael Ramsey met with Bishop Stephen Bayne and in a real sense began preparations for the third assembly of the World Council of Churches at New Delhi in November 1961 and for the tenth Lambeth Conference in 1968. Archbishop Ramsey's address at New Delhi marked him out from the outset of his primacy as a man of such stature, intellect, presence and holiness that he could easily discharge the double role of being Primate of all England and world-wide ambassador for Anglicanism both between the Churches of the Anglican Communion and in the wider ecumenical scene — not least with the Papacy and Orthodox leaders from the East.

His major address at New Delhi still stands off the page with power and significance. 'Just as our mission is unity, holiness, truth, all three,' he declared,

'so our scandal is the distortion of unity, holiness, truth, all three . . . The world does not hear the call to holiness, and does not care for the truth in Christ. But the world has its own care for unity, albeit conceived in a secular way: longing for peace, it desires that men and nations should be joined to each other and the forces which separate them removed. And the world, caring thus for unity, is shocked when the Church fails to manifest it.'[33]

Yet the 'sixties proved to be both for the Church and the world years of ferment and militancy. They were the years of campus riots of student fervour and of Vietnam. Something of this energy and challenging spirit of questioning elicited a theological liveliness both within the Church of Rome and within Anglicanism — notably within the Church of England. In 1962 the Vatican Council began amazing reforms which in their turn opened doors and windows which had been securely locked and barred since the time of the Reformation. Dr Hans Küng emerged as an international voice in the name of reformed Roman Catholic theology. They were dazzling days indeed, which saw the publication of *Soundings* edited by Dr Vidler and above all the notorious and world-wide publication of John Robinson's *Honest to God*. Along with abrasive questioning there was a new vitality and a new confidence which seemed to promote a renewed and lively dialogue between the Church and the world. It had started with the publication of *The Phenomenon of Man* by Teilhard de Chardin in 1959 and ran amok almost throughout the 1960's with the writings of Bishop James Pike, Harvey Cox and John Robinson. Theology was fun again; it was often wild; but it was not dull and it even began to ring again with that much over-used word — relevancy.

So in a real sense the Lambeth Conference was a 'new-style' occasion when it met in 1968. There seemed to be in any case a whole new array of faces. On the English bench there was Ian Ramsey, the new Bishop of Durham; Leslie Brown, who had formerly been Archbishop of Uganda, was now at St Edmundsbury and Ipswich; Bishop John Robinson, by this time almost a household name in the Western world, would surely have something to say. Oliver Tomkins, a kind of latter-day Bishop Bell, was at Bristol, and there was Mervyn Stock-wood who had been at Southwark for nine years as the password for what came to be known as 'South Bank' religion. Graham Leonard, who over the years was to become a well-known figure in the Anglican world, was going in for his first Lambeth innings at the 1968 Conference. The Welsh and Irish churches brought a fresh flush of scholarship in the persons of Glynn Simon, Bishop of Llandaff, James McCann at Armagh and George Simms at Dublin. Henry R. McAdoo, the author of *The Spirit of Anglicanism* was now Bishop of Ossory. Stephen Bayne was well into his stride and George Appleton, an authority on non-christian religions, was Archbishop of Perth in Australia. Here was surely a good first eleven, but notice that by 1968 the bishops from the Third World developing countries had yet to make a name for themselves on the field of Lambeth.

The hundredth Archbishop of Canterbury

The year 1968 was not only, however, to be the year of Lambeth. To some extent Lambeth was overshadowed by an assembly of the World Council of Churches, at Uppsala in Sweden in July, with the theme 'Behold, I make all things new'. The word *renewal* was now, by the end of the 'sixties, very much in vogue.

Indeed, since Vatican II, renewal had become a discernible movement throughout all the Churches, gathering in momentum and radically changing the chemistry of all the major Christian traditions. Archbishop Michael Ramsey returned immediately from Uppsala to face and chair the tenth Lambeth Conference, which began on July 25th, St James' Day (significantly), with the usual service at Canterbury.

The Archbishop addressed the four hundred and fifty-nine bishops as his predecessors had done from the Chair of St Augustine. At this Conference, suffragan bishops and assistant bishops as well as diocesans attended, making the largest number of bishops ever to attend a Lambeth Conference until 1988. By including the assistant and suffragan bishops, as the Archbishop had explained at his press conference, this gave an 'increased representation to the African churches'. Now not only white faces appeared on those traditional Conference photographs of all the bishops.

There were other facts of new interest about this Conference. As the press writers were not slow to point out, it was the first 'gaiterless conference'!

> 'The debonair Bishop of Chester (Gerald Ellison) turned up in gaiters at the registration and Lord Fisher wore gaiters at the Lambeth Palace garden party, but otherwise the newspapers were correct in referring to Lambeth X as "the first gaiterless Lambeth Conference".'[34]

On a more serious note, Lambeth '68 was also 'a first' in having both consultants and observers. There were twenty-five consultants (men and women, ordained and lay) representing a formidable array of theological ability. Observers from other Churches were also welcomed to be present throughout the Conference, and Church bodies ranging from the Society of Friends to the Salvation Army, Roman Catholic and Orthodox Churches readily took up the invitation, lending a strongly ecumenical air to the whole proceedings.

> 'The idea of having Consultants and Observers proved to be a huge success. The twenty-five Consultants found themselves in great demand at the meetings of Sections and Sub-Committees, as did the sixty or so Observers from other Churches, who did much more than merely observe, and gladly accepted the invitation to participate in the discussion and the debates at every level. It is probably true to say, in fact, that the level of speeches in plenary sessions from the Consultants was higher than that of the episcopal speeches, but that is no criticism of the bishops. The Consultants, after all, were specially chosen for their expertise — which the Observers also manifested — while the bishop is, and ought to be, a general practitioner.'[35]

But there was also perhaps a more significant 'first' at Lambeth 1968. When the business began, Bishop Willebrands, head of the Vatican's Secretariat for promoting Christian unity, read a special message received from the Pope. 'Never before had a Lambeth Conference been so honoured'[36] — a long cry indeed from that first tentative Conference of 1867.

This message threw into higher relief the recently issued Papal encyclical, *Humanae Vitae,* which had reiterated a prohibition on all artificial methods of birth control. Naturally the Lambeth Conference had to address this issue. At a press conference, Archbishop Ramsey reaffirmed Resolution 115 from the 1958 Conference, making quite clear that the teaching of the Anglican Communion on this matter differed very strongly from the teaching of the Papacy.

The Royal Garden Party at Buckingham Palace is always an essential part of Lambeth Conferences, and that of 1968 proved to be no exception in its colour, dress and pageantry.

'The observer from the World Methodist Council chose a black cassock, but the Bishop of Milwaukee dressed in a business suit and grey top coat. One of the Japanese bishops wore a pinkish cassock with a discernible flower pattern and slit at the side in the style of the Far East. African bishops had floppy-brimmed businessmen's hats and long overcoats that contrasted oddly with their cassocks. One bishop turned up wearing a mortarboard. The most striking costume among the women was the kimono of pale green and gold worn by the wife of the Bishop of Tokyo.'[37]

But then Anglicans pride themselves on their diversity of colourings, pluralism and comprehensiveness.

The '68 Conference had been exceptionally well prepared with a substantial volume entitled *Lambeth Conference 1968 Preparatory Information.* This proved to be an invaluable piece of work, produced largely under the direction of Bishop Ralph Dean. This volume gave full statistics on the Anglican Communion, a chapter on liturgical revisions since 1958 throughout the Communion and then a long section giving the details of statements from previous Conferences on matters already placed on the agenda for 1968. The '68 Conference was further characterized by the large number of small committees which encouraged many more of the bishops to speak and participate in the Conference — at least at this level, even if they felt constrained to more modest silence in the large and somewhat daunting plenary sessions.

Lambeth Conferences and Renewal in the Church

Renewal, as at Uppsala, in the 1968 Conference was a recurring word throughout the agenda which was divided into three parts:

The renewal of the Church in faith.
The renewal of the Church in ministry.
The renewal of the Church in unity.

Throughout long days of debate and discussions, there was only one really unpleasant occasion, and ironically it came over the question of unity — Anglican-Methodist relations in England. Resolutions and counter-resolutions crossed the floor until Archbishop de Mel, the designated preacher for the final service at St Paul's, accused the resolution over the name of Archbishop Simms of being 'a toothless, bloodless, colourless thing . . . A little more of this behaviour, and the Anglican Communion will get such a magnificent reputation for double talk that we will become utterly disreputable. Our very honour will be challenged,' he concluded, sitting down to the loudest round of applause of the whole Conference.[38]

Bishop Trevor Huddleston called de Mel's words 'utterly unchristian'; they were condemned by Bishop Russell, Assistant Bishop of Zanzibar, and Bishop Eastaugh of Peterborough, who wrote an outraged letter to the *Church Times*.

However, the overall feelings of the Conference were positive and definitely in favour of the continuation of the tradition, speaking of 'the historic importance of the Lambeth Conference over the past hundred years' and 'the undoubted value' of the '68 occasion. They requested that the 'Archbishop of Canterbury, on the advice of the Anglican Consultative Council, should call future Conferences setting their time, place and agenda.' Note the place of the newly formed Anglican Consultative Council. This replaced the long-established Lambeth Consultative Council and the more recent Anglican Council on Missionary Strategy.

Unlike previous Lambeth Conferences the 1968 Conference did not endorse any long encyclical letter. Instead, the steering committee produced a short message. Unfortunately when the message was read out 'it was greeted with but perfunctory applause.'[39] Reluctantly, the bishops voted their approval of the somewhat impotent document, with but one hand held up in objection — that of the notorious and remarkable episcopal gadfly, Dr Mervyn Stockwood of Southwark.[40]

The 1968 Conference gained much for the quite remarkable, saintly and scholarly oversight of the hundredth Archbishop of Canterbury. 'It was the first time' (and one might add probably the last time) 'that the Conference had been presided over by a theologian since Frederick Temple or Edward White Benson.'[41] There can be no doubt that Archbishop Ramsey's place in the history of the Church of England and the Anglican Communion marked quite a distinctive posture and position for Anglicanism, both in relation to the other major Churches and also in the continuing line of scholarship, stretching back through the Caroline and Elizabethan Divines — still discernible and distinctive through Bishop Gore and Archbishop William Temple, up to the close of the twentieth century.

The 'anonymous' writer of the Preface to *Crockford's* in 1987 went so far as to say that the

'last real exponent of classical Anglican divinity was Archbishop Michael Ramsey whose many scholarly studies represent a last stand before the citadel fell to the repeated assaults of the younger generation of academics.'[42]

Perhaps the essential genius (and indeed Anglican) attribute of Archbishop Michael Ramsey was his ability to combine both the role of theologian and churchman and also his devotion to the teaching of scripture, together with a real commitment to the tradition, teaching and life of the Church.

Yet in spite of this the Conference had little of any substantial theological significance to give as guidelines to the Anglican Communion on the vexed question of the ordination of women. It had refused to endorse the belief that there were no theological objections to such ordinations, yet before the next Lambeth Conference it was to be a *fait accompli* in America, leaving only the task of accommodating the novel reality by taking it into our Anglican (if not our theological) system.

The first residential Lambeth Conference

The meeting of the Anglican Consultative Council in Trinidad in

1976 could not resist the temptation to debate and discuss yet further the pros and cons of another Lambeth Conference, provisionally scheduled for 1978. Should it be another conference of the same pattern as 1968 or should there be something more synodical in structure – a kind of pan-Anglican gathering? After much talk it was decided to go again for the traditional Lambeth pattern, but with one radical and important modification. Lambeth Conferences had clearly outgrown Lambeth Palace and in 1968 had begun to use Church House, Westminster. For 1978 it was decided to go for a residential conference – the first of its kind.

In fact, the 1978 Conference was smaller in number (only four hundred and ten bishops attending in all) as suffragans and assistant bishops were excluded this time. There were also twenty consultants and about thirty-five observers from other Churches. There was to be a large number of small groups constituting the Conference and wives (under the keen eye of Mrs Jean Coggan) would be present.

For the first time simultaneous language translation facilities were made available so that 'everyone might hear the works of God in their own tongue'. There were to be fewer, shorter, and simpler resolutions as characteristic of Archbishop Coggan's Lambeth. Donald Coggan was a very different president and chairman at Lambeth '78. His predecessors had to a greater or lesser extent managed to dominate their Conferences either by the weight of their office or the sheer weight of their presence and scholarship – or all three. Donald Coggan displayed little, if any, of these characteristics. He clearly preferred to be just *primus inter pares,* as on the first day:

> 'the purple clad figure of Donald Coggan moved from the platform to the small console piano. He began the hymn, "Blest are the pure in heart", strong on the bass line. It was another footnote for the history books – the day the Archbishop of Canterbury played the piano for Evensong.'[43]

Nevertheless, Archbishop Coggan was his own man; a somewhat stern and severe evangelical, he took as his text at the opening service in Canterbury Cathedral Psalm 85 verse 8: 'I will hearken what the Lord God will say.' Strangely he shunned the use of either of the two pulpits when giving his sermon and seemed ill at ease in using the Cathedra (Augustine's seat) for its proper purpose – presiding and proclaiming. Yet the content of his opening address lacked nothing in its forcefulness, its power and its authority. He challenged the assembled bishops from the outset, staring hard through his steel-rimmed glasses and with his somewhat professorial style of delivery.

God 'spoke in the Word made Flesh' the Archbishop reassured the Lambeth Fathers. 'We have preached sermons on that', he somewhat condescendingly reminded them. 'He spoke in the formulations of the Creeds. But does he speak to us today?' he asked the bishops. Fortunately only silence met his rhetorical question. 'That is a very different matter', he continued. 'Some of us have virtually given up believing that he does, God forgive us. We would not admit it; it would shock our congregations if we did. But we have stopped listening, and our spiritual lives have died on us, though we keep up appearances and go through the motions.'[44] Brave words from an archbishop to fellow archbishops and bishops.

Before the Conference had formally begun there had been a gathering of bishops from all over the world to celebrate the charismatic renewal which had become increasingly evident in all the Churches over the previous decade, not least in the Churches of the Anglican Communion. Not many days earlier bishops and archbishops had danced in that same cathedral in the discovery of a new joy and a new love in believing. Many present hearing Archbishop Coggan on that day could therefore speak of personal renewal in their own lives of discipleship. Significantly 'The Holy Spirit and the Church today' was a committee under the first main section of the Conference entitled — 'What is the Church for?' Furthermore, Metropolitan Anthony Bloom's daily meditations during the first week of Lambeth 'did much to dissolve the resentment some bishops initially felt at being subjected to devotional lectures instead of being allowed to discuss issues they had travelled hundreds of miles to consider.'[45]

Assessing the '78 Lambeth Conference

The Conference worked hard and well. The number of agendas and quantity of paper seemed larger than ever before. Inevitably the question of women in the priesthood (now a numerous reality) produced a lengthy and complicated resolution, rewriting theology and theory around the practice of such ordinations, yet giving no guidelines as to how Anglicans might live (let alone make their communion) in a Church where opinions and practices were still strongly divided. The anxiety and diversity of practice on this matter was recognized — yet another element in Anglican comprehensiveness. However, pluralism and comprehensiveness would from now onwards necessarily relate to more than merely doctrinal matters. Church order and communion discipline are diverse in twentieth century Anglicanism and it is unlikely that it will ever be any different. If the Anglican Communion were to continue to affirm unity within diversity, there was a crying need at the Conference of 1978 to explore some guidelines for the future. Professor John Macquarrie, one of the consultants, came to the rescue of the Conference with his Scottish accent and dulcet tones when he began to speak of an 'hierarchy of truths'. He drew a helpful distinction between matters which 'made' the Church as opposed to those matters which could 'unmake' the Church. While helpful, it is doubtful whether this discussion went far enough in really practical and useful guidelines for living with a deep diversity in such matters as church order and communion discipline.

Homosexuality (notably mentioned for the first time yet chronologically before the known advent of AIDS) gets a first mention in Lambeth Conference Resolutions. The resolution has dated perhaps more than most in its necessary ignorance of the onset of AIDS and in the light both of extended debate in the General Synod of the Church of England and statements issuing from the Diocese of Newark in the United States. All this within the single decade between the 1978 Conference and 1988.

There was a helpful resolution in 1978 about the role and office of the bishop and a caution expressed about the possibility of consecrating women bishops. Here again Lambeth deliberations were rapidly dated by events and the mounting pressures which led up to the Lambeth Conference of 1988. The '78 Conference, however, counselled that although member Churches of the Anglican Communion

'may wish to consecrate a woman to the episcopate, and accepting that such a member Church must act in accordance with its own constitution, the Conference recommends that no decision to consecrate be taken without consultation with the episcopate through the primates and overwhelming support in any member Church and in the diocese concerned, lest the bishop's office should become a cause of disunity instead of a focus of unity.'[46]

On the ecumenical front, the most notable statement in '78 recognized with gratitude the setting up of the Anglican-Roman Catholic International Commission after Lambeth 1968 and urged forward this important work. Rightly discerned for what it was (and also for what it was not), Lambeth '78 was probably better placed than many of its predecessors. Since 1948 and the work of Geoffrey Fisher, independent Churches within the Anglican Communion have tested their wings and have flown, as they should, from the nest. The nature of the Lambeth Conference has therefore changed somewhat. There was even open talk in 1978 of holding future Lambeth Conferences in another Province. Certainly the feeling that Lambeth Conferences contribute a kind of international House of Bishops belonging to a pan-Anglican Synod has lessened, while the concept of worldwide episcopal consultation has grown.

It was as such a consultation that Lambeth '78 did well. Yet it was not without its detractors. The preface to 1987 *Crockford's* was strongly critical:

'Perhaps the signal example of the failure of Anglicans to deal with the question of authority was that of the Lambeth Conference of 1978. It is now generally admitted that it was poorly prepared for, indifferently led, and heavily under the influence of consultants who had not themselves thought through the ecclesiological implications of the advice they gave . . .'

Rather negatively and somewhat presumptuously, the writer concludes:

'the unimpressive performance of the Lambeth Conference in 1978 could well be attributed to lack of preparation and an urge to hasty compromise in the face of serious disagreement, but it can also be seen as a sign of a more fundamental malaise in Anglicanism, for it cannot be denied that the last thirty years have seen a significant erosion of those very factors which once created unity within such a diverse Communion.'[47]

On a lighter note, 1978 was for Bishop Mervyn Stockwood his second Lambeth Conference. Although with his characteristic genius for hospitality he entertained a very large number of the bishops at his home in Streatham, London, he was determined from the outset to attend as little of the Conference as possible. Conveniently and skilfully he arranged to be on the rota to serve in the House of Lords for almost the whole of Lambeth. When the Lords adjourned at the end of the session 'he finally put in an appearance', but 'was reported as saying somewhat wearily that he had "heard it all before".'[48]

The Bishop of London, Graham Leonard, reflecting on the Conferences of 1968 and 1978 in which he took an active part, said especially of 1978 that the

> 'agenda was totally unrealistic and the range of subjects too many to be tackled seriously. Often we were handed a draft report which we were simply expected to reaffirm — until in '78 we decided to tear it up and start again.'

He, like many of the bishops, felt that conferences of such size and numbers would do better to 'isolate an issue' and really work at it. Other bishops had similar feelings:

> 'The bishops had grown increasingly restive as their structured days passed. Spontaneity and opportunities for wide ranging debate appeared to be suppressed; they felt they were approving resolutions framed in advance, and, generally, were marking time. To many the whole Conference schedule seemed overly idealistic. "Impossible really, childish, amateurish, insulting, enormously wasteful", was the way one bishop characterized it. "All very disappointing", said the Bishop of Texas. Others said outrightly that there was definite manipulation by the ACC, its desire being to get on with things once the Lambeth Conference, which it had not wanted in the first place, was out of the way.'[49]

Presumably similar feelings were reflected in the action of Bishop John Allin, when he asked for special permission to address the Conference.

> 'The Presiding Bishop of the United States, uh, I mean in the Episcopal Church of the United States', Coggan said as Bishop Allin approached the platform. Allin asked, with his usual courtesy and typical humility, on behalf of the United States bishops

(some hundred in number and by a long way the largest single national delegation) whether there might be a re-shuffling of the Conference schedule to allow more time for input in the smaller group meetings. (Nearby, seated at the Presidential table, neither Coggan nor Howe could quite mask their annoyance.) There was no discussion, and the motion was carried at once. The Conference applauded again as though cheered by evidence that for the first time it appeared to be at least partially in control of its life.'[50]

'Some Third World bishops lost hope, both in listening and speaking. "The rules of debate had them at sea", said Mercer of Matabeleland. One Ugandan said to a Consultant, "This is not our way of doing things, so we just leave you to it."'[51]

With a few notable exceptions much of the drafting was the work of the English and American bishops, who still (almost inevitably) tended to dominate, especially in the plenary sessions.

There was a strange note of irony both about the '68 and '78 Conferences. Outside events somewhat dominated the media on both occasions: in 1968, the Pope published his controversial encyclical, *Humanae Vitae*, and in 1978 he died. The timing in both cases was either disastrous or brilliant, depending on how you happened to see it all.

Is there a future for Lambeth Conferences?

So what of Lambeth Conferences? What have they achieved? Ought they to continue? In a sense, to attempt to answer these questions is to cheat at this stage of the book, rather like turning to the last chapter half-way through the detective story to find out who did it. Certainly much can be said which is favourable about the record of Lambeth Conferences. Like many excellent things, we may have to say of Lambeth Conferences that if they did not exist we would probably have had to invent them — or something very similar to them. The unity which binds together the independent Provinces is, to say the least, a subtle and fragile one. Yet, given the dispersed nature of authority in Anglicanism, the Lambeth Conference should never seek inappropriate muscle nor streamline or centralize that authority in anything more than an episcopal fellowship or *philadelphia* which is clearly the main emphasis in Lambeth gatherings at their best.

'If it had said less,' said Archbishop Lang's biographer, reflecting on the Lambeth Conference of 1930, 'it would have said very little; and if it had tried to say more, it might have ended by saying nothing.'[52] Probably much the same could be said, not totally negatively, about all Lambeth Conferences.

The arguments in favour of a gathering more in line with a pan-Anglican synod are somewhat more formidable to contemplate. The laity and clergy who serve on national synods tend (perhaps necessarily) to be unrepresentative. The mind boggles at the kind of people who would come to the front to sit in such a pan-Anglican synod. Church 'hobbyists' have tended to corner national synodical power, playing ecclesiastical politics and apeing rather poorly secular forms of democratic government. Whereas the bishop or the apostle by his calling and office has been specially set aside to be, by grace (not necessarily by nature) a truly representative person. Furthermore, in the Ordinal, the ministry and mission of a bishop, while relating very closely to his diocese, is also seen, at least in terms of the Prayer Book, as exercising that ministry and mission throughout the world. 'As a chief pastor he shares with his fellow bishops a special responsibility to maintain and further the unity of the Church, to uphold its discipline, and to guard its faith.'[53] It is difficult to see how he can do that unless from time to time he is ready to give time to being present at gatherings in fellowship with other bishops throughout the world and to take counsel concerning common problems and difficulties. St Augustine of Hippo, who had a high doctrine of the commitment of the bishop to his diocese and who also incidentally disliked travel intensely, nevertheless saw his participation in the Councils of Bishops as part of his vocation and calling. He regularly attended the Councils gathered in Carthage and elsewhere in the larger life of the African Church. It is perhaps not to make too high a claim if we say that a bishop by the grace of his office has a special charism (discernment) for this important aspect of his work.

It is right that over the years the work of Lambeth gatherings has been supplemented by the Anglican Consultative Council (somewhat synodical in representation and structure) and also latterly by the meetings of the Primates. It is right that Lambeth Conferences should be supplemented by these kinds of agencies: it is almost certainly wrong if ever they were supplanted.

'Lambeth Conferences,' maintains Bishop Jenkins of Durham, 'are really something of an historical accident, (as is indeed the Anglican Communion itself) . . . If it had courage it could do great things.'

And where should these Conferences be held? There is marginally more to be said in favour of returning to Canterbury for these occasions than in selecting some other location. Christianity and tradition are essentially sacramental — they are tied to geography. The Anglican Communion must not degenerate into just an idea. If it is a reality it is sacramental, or as one bishop who had served in Africa said more simply, 'You need to be able to touch it.' Perhaps Archbishop Michael Ramsey was saying more than he realized when he spoke on the subject of things and places and the power which places have to represent symbolically and sacramentally the intangible realities of which they are but symbols and signs. 'Here comes the great principle,' he said in his inimitable tones at the opening of the '78 Lambeth Conference. 'Here comes the great principle — because things are not to be loved for the sake of places, but places for the sake of good things. (*Non pro locis res, sed pro bonis rebus loca amanda sunt.*) How suggestive', he went on,

> 'how far reaching is the principle, how applicable to other issues and to other times. The local, the limited, the particular is to be cherished by Christian people, not for any nostalgic attachment to it for its own sake, but always for the *real thing* which it represents and conveys, the thing which is catholic, essential, lasting. So our love for Canterbury melts into our love for Christ whose shrine Canterbury is; our love for what is Anglican is a little piece of our love for One, Holy, Catholic, Apostolic Church.'[54]

Neither Lambeth Conferences as such nor Canterbury as such are catholic, essential or lasting in themselves, yet by God's grace and generosity what they have come to represent over the years is hopefully and most necessarily catholic, essential and lasting.

'There is a necessity of an institution to be visible', said Bishop John Klyberg, formerly from Zambia. 'People need to feel a part of it, to be able to touch it — it can't be an institution just on paper ... . They' (the African Churches), he concluded, 'were strongly opposed to the

31

Lambeth '78 suggestion to have the Conference removed away from Canterbury.'

In 1930, T.S. Eliot wrote a small work entitled, *Thoughts After Lambeth.* 'The Church of England washes its dirty linen in public . . . In contrast to some other institutions, both civil and ecclesiastical, the linen does get washed.'[55] For, like all human effort at working out the divine will, we must always let God be God, which means we have to live with that double and seemingly contradictory injunction (also from the pen of T.S. Eliot) 'to care and not to care'. Unless we can laugh to some extent at our family gatherings, we shall grow solemn and they will become joyless with light falling away from them. Then something worse can happen: they become idols which we fail to see *through.* All our best undertakings are intended to be only icons and the essential point of icons is that they do not lose their power to point us beyond themselves, as we see through them to something even greater which is always beyond them. What we see *through* them is always something more — the infinite *through* the finite — the universal *through* the particular and local. What we see through them is just a little of that vision which Isaiah saw through the smoke and the shaking of the temple on its very shaky foundations. What we see is God who alone is our rock and our stronghold. Nothing, nothing must displace that reality which alone is eternal and infinite, in a word — Jesus is Lord (even of Lambeth Conferences) because God reigns. The words of Archbishop William Temple, preaching at one particular Lambeth Conference (1930), ring true and because they ring true could be — and indeed should be — applied not only to all Lambeth Conferences but to all our deliberations, our yearnings and our searchings as the people of God.

Temple concluded his fine sermon at the opening of that Conference with these words:

'While we deliberate, He reigns; when we decide wisely, He reigns; when we decide foolishly, He reigns; when we serve Him in humble loyalty, He reigns; when we serve Him self-assertively, He reigns; when we rebel and seek to withhold our service, He reigns — the Alpha and the Omega which is, and which was, and which is to come, the Almighty.'[56]
Amen.

REFERENCES

[1] R.T. Davidson, *Life of Archibald Campbell Tait, Archbishop of Canterbury,* Macmillan & Co., London, 1891, Volume II, p. 366

[2] J.G. Lockhart, *Cosmo Gordon Lang,* Hodder & Stoughton, Ltd., London, 1949, p. 344

[3] Ibid., p. 344

[4] Ibid., p. 345

[5] Crockford's *Clerical Directory,* 1975, preface

[6] J.G. Lockhart, *Cosmo Gordon Lang,* Hodder & Stoughton Ltd., London, 1949, p. 344

[7] John Howe, *Highways and Hedges: Anglicanism and the Universal Church,* Anglican Book Centre, Toronto, Ontario, 1985, p. 100

[8] Alan M.G. Stephenson, *The First Lambeth Conference 1867,* S.P.C.K., London, 1967, p. 160

[9] Randall T. Davidson (Ed.), *The Lambeth Conferences of 1867, 1878 and 1888,* S.P.C.K., London 1889, p 34 ff

[10] R.T. Davidson, *Life of Archibald Campbell Tait, Archbishop of Canterbury,* Macmillan & Co., London, 1891, Volume II, p. 376

[11] William Purcell, *Fisher of Lambeth,* Hodder & Stoughton, 1969, p. 186

[12] Ibid., p 200

[13] Ibid., p. 174

[14] Ibid., p. 176

[15] Frank Longford, *The Bishops, A Study of Leaders in the Church Today,* Sidgwick & Jackson, London, 1986, p. 27

[16] David L. Edwards, *Christian England,* William B. Eerdmans Publishing Co., Grand Rapids, MI, 1984, Vol. 3, p. 212

[17] F.L. Cross, *The Oxford Dictionary of the Christian Church,* Oxford University Press, London, 1957, p. 820

[18] S.C. Carpenter, *Church and People 1789-1889,* S.P.C.K., London, 1959, Vol. 3, p. 441

[19] Owen Chadwick, *The Victorian Church,* Adam and Charles Black, London, 1970, p. 336

[20] Ibid.

[21] R.T. Davidson, *Life of Archibald Campbell Tait, Archbishop of Canterbury,* Macmillan & Co., London, 1891, Vol. II,

p. 337

[22] Ibid., p. 367

[23] Ibid.

[24] Ibid.

[25] Ibid., p. 369

[26] Ibid, p. 376

[27] Edward Carpenter, *Cantuar: The Archbishops in Their Office,* Cassell, London, 1971, p. 335

[28] Ibid., p 487 ff

[29] William Purcell, *Fisher of Lambeth,* Hodder & Stoughton, London, 1969, p. 283

[30] Alan M.G. Stephenson, *Anglicanism and the Lambeth Conferences,* S.P.C.K., London, p. 214 ff

[31] Ibid.

[32] Ibid.

[33] Ibid., p. 217

[34] James B. Simpson and Edward M. Story, *The Long Shadows of Lambeth X,* McGraw-Hill Book Co., 1969, p. 22

[35] Alan M.G. Stephenson, *Anglicanism and the Lambeth Conferences,* S.P.C.K., London, p. 237

[36] Ibid., p. 241

[37] James B. Simpson and Edward M. Story, *The Long Shadows of Lambeth X,* McGraw-Hill Book CO., 1969, p. 93

[38] Alan M.G. Stephenson, *Anglicanism and the Lambeth Conferences,* S.P.C.K., London, p. 255

[39] Alan M.G. Stephenson, *Anglicanism and the Lambeth Conferences,* S.P.C.K., London, p. 255

[40] Ibid.

[41] Ibid.

[42] Crockford's *Clerical Directory*

[43] James B. Simpson and Edward M. Story, *Discerning God's Will,* Thomas Nelson, 1979, p. 30

[44] Ibid., p. 260 ff

[45] Ibid., p. 225

[46] Ibid., p. 308 ff.

[47] Crockford's *Clerical Directory,* 1987, p. 62

[48] James B. Simpson and Edward M. Story, *Discernng God's Will,* Thomas Nelson, 1979, p. 217

[49] Ibid., p. 210

[50] Ibid., p. 149

[51] Ibid., p. 213

[52] J.G. Lockhart, *Cosmo Gordon Lang,* Hodder & Stoughton Ltd., London, 1949, p. 354

[53] *The Alternative Service Book 1980,* Hodder & Stoughton, The Ordinal, p. 388

[54] James B. Simpson and Edward M. Story, *The Long Shadows of Lambeth X,* McGraw-Hill Book Co., 1969, p. 282 ff

[55] J.G. Lockhart, *Cosmo Gordon Lang,* Hodder & Stoughton Ltd., London, 1949, p. 354

[56] F.A. Iremonger, *William Temple, Archbishop of Canterbury, His Life and Letters,* Oxford University Press, 1949, p. 459

CHAPTER TWO

The Spirit of Anglicanism and the Ghosts of Lambeth

> *'Its influence is great, its prestige is enormous.' Anglicanism 'is the pioneer of ecumenism with its Lambeth Quadrilateral; and it is receptive to what is happening in other Churches. It has respect for the historic Churches; a loyalty to man as man, and the constituted public order; a sensitivity to the social problems and sufferings of man; a zeal for evangelization and pastoral care; a concern for mission; a sacramental and historic catholicity, with evangelical reform: an awareness of interdependence in Christ's Body; an incarnate and contextualized liturgy; a loyalty to the Church without dogmatic pressures.'*
>
> Bishop Adrián Cáceres[1]

Diversity, toleration and unity

The scene is the library in the great hall at Lambeth Palace. The year is 1878. Exactly one hundred bishops are crowded into that library which is sometimes called Juxon's Hall (after the name of the archbishop who spent so much time, money and energy on restoring it). The bishops are dressed largely in frock coats and gaiters — the latter looking more decorative on some legs than on others! The assembly is being addressed by an old and somewhat sad man, who had lost his son at the tender age of twenty-eight only weeks before. Yet there was power and presence in the old man's presentation, tinged now though with a sadness to which he permits himself occasionally to refer, yet always with that restraint for which the English, the Empire and the age of Victoria are all equally noted.

Archbishop Archibald Campbell Tait, formerly headmaster of Rugby School and subsequently Bishop of London, was both a statesman and a broad churchman. He did not lean too much toward the powerful and zealous party of evangelicals which had emerged and evolved during the nineteenth century nor did he favour the tractarians or catholic wing of the Church which had grown in influence and numbers since the days of 1832, the Oxford Movement, and such notable preachers, pastors and priests as Newman, Pusey and Keble.

After much goading (largely from the Episcopal Church in America) and with the support of the Convocations of York and Canterbury, Archbishop Tait had somewhat tentatively issued an invitation to the Anglican bishops worldwide to attend a second Lambeth Conference.

There had been, three days earlier, an impressive sermon in Canterbury Cathedral, when Archbishop Tait addressed the bishops – significantly, from the Chair of St Augustine. He was in every way a man of larger stature and larger horizons than his predecessor, another ex-headmaster (Harrow), Archbishop Longley.

Archbishop Tait, during his fourteen years as archbishop, established the office of Primate of All England on a new and higher prominence than it had known for a long time. At the end of his Primacy in 1882 it was said 'by more than one – some of them not altogether friendly to the Church – that the Chair of Canterbury has never stood so high as it does now for two hundred and fifty years.'[2]

It was this archbishop who, in Lambeth's great hall and library, surveyed the faces of his fellow bishops. Some of them were from Churches which represented the distinctively more catholic wing of Anglicanism of which he somewhat disapproved. These infant Churches in their far-flung dioceses had cut loose from the British establishment, Parliament and the Monarch. They felt free to try their wings, thus enlarged and coloured by more catholic and 'high church' practices. The other developing wing in Anglicanism since the 1830's had been the evangelical wing, with its powerful emphasis upon lay-witness in the persons of such people as William Wilberforce who had struggled for the abolition of slavery across the road in the larger and more impressive halls of Parliament. For the Church in England after two centuries of largely latitudinarian and broad church dominance, was extending the ends of its spectrum and beginning to feel the strains of being a multi-dimensional Church.

Surely, then, it was something of this that Tait had in mind when he looked across the rows of episcopal faces 'back home from the colonies' and addressed them in long and weighty words. He was facing the diversity, pluralism and tensions of Anglicanism, albeit on a comparatively small scale, yet the gathering on that day represented evolution, change and the beginnings of comprehensiveness on a scale hitherto inapparent and much less threatening.

'We have no power to bind anybody,' the Archbishop tactfully reminded himself and his brother bishops, 'and we do not desire to have it. The very diversity of our constitutions, the very differences of climate and of civil government in the countries from which we come, remind us that we must be prepared for diversity' (there comes the word) 'in the midst of essential union. Outside the Church we must be prepared to be tolerant even though we do not receive toleration in return. This sort of toleration for which I plead is a Christian virtue and it is not less for us a Christian virtue because other men choose to ignore it. This toleration is the same as catholicity. Sects are narrow and intolerant. The catholic church of Christ is wide and knows no intolerance. . . . Brethren' he concluded, 'we want no new gospel, but we want the old one more distinctly and clearly proclaimed in its entirety.'[3]

In many ways, and in ways which Tait could not possibly have foreseen, he was setting the scene and indeed the conference agenda for Anglicanism (and for future Lambeths) for the next hundred and ten years up to and including the Lambeth Conference of 1988.

'The Nature of the Unity We Seek'

The scene is a large gymnasium in the University of Kent, England. The date is Monday, July 18th, 1988. The occasion is the twelfth Lambeth Conference, and the gymnasium, which has been converted to a conference hall at some expense, is now packed with well over five hundred bishops, black and white, many consultants and observers. There is a press gallery and closed-circuit television cameras relay the proceedings to a nearby lecture theatre where a further two hundred and fifty seats are provided for members of the general public who

Archbishop Runcie
Chairman 1988 Lambeth Conference

have eagerly come to listen to the opening address given by the one hundred and second successor to St Augustine — the Most Reverend and Right Honourable Robert Runcie. His topic will be, significantly, 'The Nature of the Unity We Seek'.

The Archbishop prepares to speak. He is certainly not a headmaster as many of his recent predecessors have been. He is a don, and speaks with somewhat smooth, articulate and well-manicured tones. Yet the overall effect is one of precision and strong inward conviction. A long time seems to have passed since he urged each of these assembled bishops in his invitation in 1983 to 'be in close communication with his diocese' about the twelfth Lambeth Conference, and to come to this Conference reflecting the concerns of their dioceses: 'Each bishop will bring his diocese with him', the Archbishop had urged optimistically.

Women as well as men consultants flank the rows of purple-shirted prelates, while microphones, cameras and other samples of twentieth century technology are preparing to roll and to capture the Archbishop's words for posterity, if not for the wider and larger world of his own day. Now, for the first time since the Reformation (and in ways which Tait would have abhorred) the Archbishop of Canterbury does not speak in a realistic way as head of the national Church in England, if by that we mean the Church which the majority of English men and women attend in 1988. In recent years, the Church of England has fallen on rather hard times and church attendance has shrunk dramatically. In 1988 the Church of England has marginally fewer people in all its church buildings on a Sunday than the Roman Catholic Church. That is a startling statistic. Tait had been under no misapprehension when he addressed his Lambeth Conference that he spoke as the spiritual head of a national Church which had been established by law from Tudor times.

Bring their dioceses with them? Did Runcie really mean that? The nations, dioceses and cultures represented in this conference hall are huge and diverse. Of course the Americans still represent the largest single contingent and then, not unnaturally, the Church of England (ironically one of the smaller and weaker Churches in the Anglican Communion today). Canada, Australia, and New Zealand are well represented among the assembled bishops – giving a faint echo of the days of the British Empire and the British Commonwealth which had largely dominated nineteenth century Lambeth Conferences. Yet in all, every continent in the world is represented in this assembly hall by twenty-eight provinces, four hundred and thirty dioceses and sixty-four thousand individual congregations, all from a total of one hundred and sixty-four countries. It is a nice question to ask whether Archbishop Tait would have recognized this gathering or the gathering the previous day in Canterbury Cathedral for the opening ceremony as his Anglican Church? Is this what he meant by 'diversity' and 'catholicity'? It is true that he would have known what is meant by evangelicals and ritualists, for they had emerged in his lifetime and he had sought to tame something of their excesses. Yet what would he have made of Graham Leonard, the Bishop of London? Or of Moses

Tay, the Bishop of Singapore, to say nothing of Bishop Spong of Newark, USA? What a spectrum! Diversity? Yes, indeed, and more. They are all in some sense bringing their dioceses with them but we can be certain that their agendas will vary considerably. While Bishop Spong will eagerly wish to discuss women bishops, he will also have on his agenda homosexual lifestyle, feminism and inclusive God-language. That's the kind of diversity present in this hall awaiting words from the Archbishop of Canterbury on 'The Unity We Seek'. Bishop Colin Bazley of Chile had in fact openly said before the Conference that Spong's kind of agenda meant nothing to his diocese in the part of the Church that he would be seeking to represent. He comes with an altogether different agenda:

> 'The issues of sexuality, inclusive language, women priests — these issues do not touch us in the southern hemisphere. Africa, Asia and South America have different priorities from those in the northern hemisphere.'

Then there are the many black bishops from Africa in general and from Uganda in particular with burning-hot faith, fresh from the crucible of persecution, yet with a joy and love of the Gospel (evangelical as well as catholic; Gospel *and* Church) evident in their whole bearing. Nothing very latitudinarian about these bishops. Dialogue and discussion are expensive luxuries for men like these, displaced by the more pressing needs of witness, evangelism, unity and mission in countries torn by poverty, terrorism, tyranny and warfare.

A large number of the bishops present indeed have heavy hearts. They come from countries and dioceses where famine, poverty, AIDS and disease have ravaged the land. Will Lambeth '88 have a word for them? While some bishops might come fresh from debates in their dioceses about inclusive God-language in the liturgy, other bishops like Archbishop Tutu and his bishops from South Africa will come from congregations who cannot even afford a new prayer book in their own language and where the areas of petty discussion about likes and dislikes of new prayer books would appear ludicrous and self-indulgent. Some of the bishops present at Lambeth '88 can be forgiven perhaps for some impatience with the niceties of liturgy when they come from countries torn by the evils of apartheid and racism, to say nothing of soured Church relations with other Churches and other religions. The shape of their agendas is very different indeed from the agendas that are pinned to the hearts and sleeves of some of the American and northwestern bishops.

So, translation in other languages will not be all that will be needed if the bishops in the Conference are to engage in any realistic discussion or debate. It will require nothing less than an almighty outpouring of the Holy Spirit, as at the first Pentecost, if a gathering of such diversity, different colourings and cultures stands even the remotest chance of hearing 'in their own tongue' of 'The Unity We Seek', to say nothing of 'the mighty works of God'.

It is noteworthy perhaps that if Latin has gone forever from the prayers at such formal gatherings as these, that there are several bishops in the Lambeth Conference of 1988 who will speak in tongues. Before the Conference began there had been a gathering which Archbishop Tait would certainly not have recognized as even remotely Anglican! From July the 9th to the 12th on this same university campus, a group representing renewal in Anglicanism had held a pre-Lambeth Conference with the somewhat daunting title — 'The Church in the Valley of Decision'. Such a group speaks in challenging tones about the imperative of world evangelization, the pursuit of holiness and the gifts of the spirit. As something of a new emphasis within Anglicanism, charismatics have gathered much power and recognition in recent years and it is significant that their meeting was held when and where it was. The colourings of Anglicanism are indeed diverse; Archbishop Tait in his day would probably have unchurched many who will be more comfortably recognized at this all-embracing Lambeth Conference. Such is something of the diversity of Anglicanism in 1988: little wonder then that the opening address is entitled, 'The Nature of the Unity We Seek'.

A backwards glance

Archbishop Tait may well have inquired if he had come to the right meeting. We too may ask if we have come to the right meeting. After all, this is not Lambeth Palace. Is it the same Church as the Church of Tait's day? Where is there continuity in evidence amongst such obvious discontinuity? Where is the unity amid such obvious diversity?

Perhaps as we sit back and look across the ranks of bishops assembled in Kent University gymnasium, we might allow our minds to go back again, this time to the more sombre scene of 1867 — that first Lambeth gathering. The gathering is smaller — much smaller. There are only seventy-six bishops present. Furthermore, they are white faces to a man, and of course there are no women present. (There was in fact one black bishop in the Anglican Communion in 1867, Bishop Samuel Adjai Crowther, but he was unable to attend the Lambeth Conference.)

Presiding is Archbishop Charles Longley — 'an honest man without distinguished talents.'[4] He had been very apprehensive indeed about that first Lambeth Conference. Anxieties which mounted daily as bishops like the zealous Bishop Selwyn from New Zealand and the articulate Bishop Gray of Capetown arrived in England and made their way hotfoot to Lambeth Palace with pressing agendas ready for the start of the Conference. The evening before the Conference began, the anxious Longley had taken a long walk out of the little village of Addington, near Croydon, where in those days the Archbishop still had a summer home. We are told that as Longley walked he repeated this ejaculatory prayer for the Conference: 'God is our own God, and he will give us his blessing.'[5]

For there were troubles in the air even back in those more settled days — doctrinal problems as well as difficulties about church order and discipline. Bishop Selwyn on the fourth and last day of the Conference was to leap to his feet to propose a resolution which stated that 'the whole Anglican communion is deeply injured by the present condition of the Church in Natal.' The response to such a crisis was a very Anglican response indeed — namely to set up a committee, perhaps the most persistent reflex action of Anglicanism throughout its long and checkered history! Bishop Colenso, a former maths master at Harrow School (where Longley had been headmaster) and now Bishop of Natal, was regarded by Bishop Gray of Capetown, Bishop Selwyn and many others as distinctively 'unsound' in his theology in general and un-Anglican in his biblical scholarship in particular. After all, Article VI of the Thirty-Nine Articles is perfectly clear and remarkably unequivocal: 'Holy Scripture containeth all things necessary to salvation.' Yet here was Bishop Colenso not only writing books which reflected some of the biblical criticism coming out of the German schools, but now, as Bishop of Natal, he was refusing to condemn polygamy as practiced in the tribal culture prevalent in the parts of Africa where he had recently been appointed bishop. Toleration — yes, but can or should Anglicanism or indeed Christianity tolerate that? Comprehensive, yes — but how comprehensive?

So although the dress, setting and chemistry of that first Lambeth Conference feels very different from the Conference of 1988, both Conferences share many of the same concerns and meet in a similar atmosphere of strain and tension, seeking a unity within diversity and the spirit of comprehensiveness.

Perhaps it is worth commenting at this stage that by contemporary standards, Lambeth Conferences in the past have been attended by a very learned and scholarly bevy of bishops. Professor Eric Mascall wrote in a pamphlet after the 1958 Conference that few bishops that year had much theological learning. (Perhaps 1958 was a bad year!) The same could not, however, be said of that group in 1867. 'There were notable theologians, church historians and classicists, men of legal knowledge and men of medical knowledge.'[6] Anglicanism has throughout its history been characterized by an emphasis upon sound learning. The bishops at that first Conference of 1867, though small in number, were weighty in their scholarship and learning. They were in the direct apostolic line with bishops of earlier centuries who had rightly given to the Church of England the reputation of being a Church of sound learning — a Church where reason took its place alongside tradition and scripture in a three-fold witness to the person of Christ.

Anglicanism and the Thirty-Nine Articles

On the first day of the 1867 Conference, the bishops were due to discuss 'Inter-communion between the Churches of the Anglican Communion'. The Anglican Communion had evolved from the Church of England, whose unity was guarded by the use of a prayer book enforced by the laws of Parliament and with a supreme governor in the person of the Monarch. The outline of its faith and the geography of the parameters of that faith, are to be found like signposts on the map of sixteenth-century religious controversy in the famous

Thirty-Nine Articles. In those articles the scriptures are the basis of belief, interpreted in the light of the Creeds and the Councils of the undivided Church. Yet unlike the other Reformation Churches, the Church of England has never been a confessing Church — Anglicans are not tied to any particular confession of faith. You cannot go anywhere and find a kind of theological 'Magna Carta' nor the equivalent of a kind of theological American Constitution. (The American Church above all Churches in the Anglican Communion today might find this a difficult concept, set as it is within a culture which tends to approach a written and documented constitution with an idealism bordering on idolatry.) The absence of a written constitution is of course a rather English trait, and perhaps a trait which spills over into all things Anglican — namely, to be a little suspicious of written constitutions, of paper and printed Confessions. The Thirty-Nine Articles still constitute the nearest you can get in Anglicanism to some kind of statement of an Anglican position. Nevertheless they have to be seen in their historical context. They were guidelines setting parameters to Anglican belief in a Europe which was torn apart by extremists of every theological kind. The Thirty-Nine Articles (printed in the back of every 1662 *Book of Common Prayer*) are intended as signposts marking out the central ground of faith with definite colouring at the centre and more indefinite colouring perhaps towards the edges.

However, they do not have any claim to infallibility for the Church — or for any church: 'The Church of Jerusalem, Alexandria and Antioch have erred', states Article XIX without any qualification. 'So also the Church of Rome hath erred not only in their living and manner of ceremonies, but also in matters of faith.' Yes, there is a ruthless refusal in Anglicanism at its best to exalt any of the resources of faith — whether scripture, tradition or reason — to a place of infallibility. In a sweeping assertion, the 'ever-memorable' John Hales (1584–1656) sums up the Anglican position in these important words (no less important in 1988 than in 1636 when they were first written):

> 'Infallibility either in judgement, or in interpretation, or in whatsoever, is annext neither to the See of any Bishop [Rome or Canterbury] nor to the Councils, nor to the Church, nor to any created power whatsoever.'

There it is: no *thing* created is infallible for an Anglican — not even

General Synods of the Church of England, nor national conventions of America nor indeed Lambeth Conferences. It has to be said that they can be and often are sources of real and living authority, but never are they infallible. Faith for Anglicans is a living and continuing evolution and reflection upon sources of authority, but always seen as icons, pointing beyond themselves to the only One who is infallible, namely the true and living God. There is a refusal in Anglicanism at its best to create theological idols which shut us off from living communion with that living God whose truth and light entered our dark world in the face of Jesus Christ.

Even at that first Lambeth Conference there was discussion and disagreement about the content of faith and the ordering and life of the Church — such discussion and disagreement, it would seem, are of the very chemistry of Anglicanism, and frankly it has to be said that if you find it too hot in the Lambeth 'kitchen', the Anglican Church is probably not the place for you. When those first Lambeth Fathers got down to a discussion on the General Councils of the Church (rather like discussions on the number of sacraments) they could not agree on how many they should recognize! Bishop Hopkins wanted six councils mentioned, as being a basis for authority from the days of the undivided Church. The evangelicals were from the outset uneasy about the whole question of the authority of the Councils of the Church at any time or at any place, preferring to speak only of the authority of scripture — the slogan of *sola scriptura* from Reformation days. After all, as we have seen, the one thing that the Thirty-Nine Articles promulgated about General Councils was that to a man they could all err. So it was that Bishop McIlvaine fought powerfully and somewhat cunningly for their exclusion — and excluded they were, much to the chagrin of Bishop Hopkins who 'was defeated and went home miserable.'

Hence the opening Declaration of that first Lambeth Conference reads (with something of a touch of the grandiose):

'We, Bishops of Christ's Holy Catholic Church, in visible communion with the United Church of England and Ireland, professing the faith delivered to us in Holy Scripture, maintained by the primitive Church and reaffirmed by the Fathers of the English Reformation . . .'[7]

The scene of that 1867 Conference begins to fade as we relax and reflect with its chairman who, looking back on the events of those few days, confessed that he would 'always look back on the Conference as an important era in my life and Archiepiscopate. I trust that it has tended to bind the different branches of the Church in our Anglican Communion more closely together in the bonds of brotherly love.'[8] It had done so and they (Lambeth Conferences in general) surely do. It had not solved the Colenso crisis — Lambeth Conferences seldom seem to *solve* those kinds of problems. But then from the outset Lambeth Conferences have not attempted to imitate (nor should they) ecumenical councils. The pastoral declaration and reports which have issued from successive Lambeth Conferences are not Papal bulls, nor should they claim to be, nor should they be accused of failing if they are clearly not of such pretentious proportions. So Longley wrote to his sister,

> 'If the only fruit of it (the 1867 Conference) had been that Pastoral which will be translated into Greek and Latin and circulated throughout the whole of Christendom; it would have been enough, when combined with the brotherly union of seventy-six bishops from all quarters of the globe.'[9]

However, it has to be said that such a chemistry of unity and authority is not enough for some fragile spirits. There have been and there always will be severe critics of Anglicanism. Superficially it can appear to lack backbone or to be insufficiently resilient for a climate of contention and questioning such as we experience in today's world. Timid spirits will want the truths and proclamations from Lambeth Conferences to be carved in stone and set up like an obelisk, demanding not only our attention and reflection, but also more subtly our worship — a worship which is due only to God made known to us in the personal revelation of Jesus Christ.

Such a mentality had been catered for only a few years before that first Lambeth Conference, in the Papal Bull of 1854 concerning the Immaculate Conception of Our Lady and again in the Syllabus of Errors of 1864. Compared with such statements and bulls, Longley's Lambeth Declaration may seem all too unpretentious — but then such a comparison, in spite of the words of the versifier in the *Punch* of Longley's day, is really like a comparison of apples and oranges:

'To grow an Ox the Frog did blow
himself in vain to bursting full;
and Canterbury does just so,
trying to match the Papal Bull.'[10]

Whatever Anglicanism is or is not, it most certainly is not modelled on the structures of the Roman Catholic Church with its head office in Rome (or Canterbury, Jerusalem or Constantinople or anywhere else on earth) and its 'branch offices' scattered around the world. In 1988 there are twenty-eight Churches which make up that Anglican Communion of which Archbishop Longley spoke with such concern in 1867. One of them (possibly the weakest while being the oldest) is the Church of England. 'The Anglican Communion is not an organization by which older and stronger Churches can extend their influence over younger and weaker Churches', said Bishop Stephen Bayne at the Anglican Congress in Toronto, Canada, in 1963.

> 'We are not interested in branch offices around the world. We care rather for a household within which many Churches, representing many cultures and peoples, can take their self-reliant and buoyant place in full brotherhood, each giving and teaching, each receiving and learning. Therefore our organization must both reflect this and nourish it.'[11]

In many ways the organization of the Anglican Communion reflects the autocephelous (self-heading) Orthodox Churches of the East, which are a much closer model for Anglicanism than the model of the Roman Catholic Church.

Earlier battles in Anglicanism

But now we must let our minds go back further still in our picture of Anglicanism, to its roots and eventually to the acorn from which the tree of Anglicanism has grown and evolved. The scene is still Lambeth Palace. The year is 1633. William Laud, the seventy-seventh Archbishop of Canterbury, is moving into Lambeth Palace, complete with two pets — a tortoise and a Smyrna cat. His move across the River Thames to Lambeth was somewhat unfortunate to say the least. The ferry carrying him, his coach and horses capsized on the Thames endangering life and limb. 'But I praise God for it, I lost neither man nor horse.'[12] Laud did not enjoy his life at Lambeth with the prospect of 'slid(ing) over in a barge to the Court and the Star Chamber' as he frequently had to do during his years as Archbishop of Canterbury. He had infinitely preferred living on the north side of the river, where the seat of secular power was situated and where in the course of his political and ecclesiastical ascendancy he had jolted in that same coach, presumably, 'over the stones between London House and Whitehall'.

Yet for Archbishop Laud there was no need to be concerned about the Church's sources of authority and unity, for since the stormy days of the Reformation and the Elizabethan settlement much had changed: 'The Church and the State,' he wrote, 'are so near united and knit together, that though they may seem two bodies, yet indeed in some relations they may be accounted as but one.'[13] The state, and especially the person of the monarch, would insure from Archbishop Laud's point of view all the unity within and conformity of the Church of England to its own beliefs — not least in its worship, its rites and its ceremonies. Truth to tell, Archbishop Laud attempted to impose upon Anglicanism the sort of unity and uniformity for which it had never been built. The Preface to the *Book of Common Prayer* and certainly the spirit of the Elizabethan settlement, in the face of the bloodiest of disunity in the middle of the sixteenth century, had deliberately set the feet of Anglicanism within a large room with these famous words:

> 'It hath been the wisdom of the Church of England, ever since the first compiling of her Publick Liturgy, to keep the mean between the two extremes, of too much stiffness in refusing, and of too much easiness in admitting any variation from it.'

Archbishop Laud genuinely believed that in his day there was 'too much easiness in admitting' variation (largely puritanical) from the norm (especially in worship) established in the Prayer Book of Elizabeth in 1559. The Act of Uniformity was on the statute book and to that act and its political power Laud intended to appeal. First and foremost his appeal was to the King (in his mind clearly *above* Parliament) as both supreme governor of the Church of England by law established and also the bearer of that proud title (first given to Henry

VIII by no less a person than the Pope himself) — 'Defender of the Faith'. (Incidentally that title is still proudly carried by the monarch of England to this day and is reproduced on many British coins.) Yet Laud was threatening by this kind of behaviour not only to overturn the barge that brought him to Lambeth but also to overturn the ship of the Church itself, which had weathered so well the stormy waters of the Reformation in the previous century. After all, did not Article XXXIV explicitly say:

> 'It is not necessary that Traditions and Ceremonies be in all places one, and utterly like: for at all times they have been diverse, and may be changed according to the diversities of countries, times, and men's manners.'

The same Article goes even further — as though it could already see something of the diverse customs, rites and ceremonies of the member Churches of the Anglican Communion in our day which did not emerge or evolve until several centuries after Article XXXIV had been written: 'Every particular or national Church hath authority to ordain, change, and abolish, ceremonies or rites of the Church.' Yes — but notice (and of course this is the grit in the oyster of all discussions before the sixteenth century and since) — only such rites and ceremonies as have been 'ordained only by man's authority'. And furthermore, all changes must not be 'against God's Word'. Oh yes, there are parameters, lines and edges in the features of Anglicanism and perhaps all of them should be re-examined in the light of twentieth century discussions and controversies.

This kind of comprehensiveness is both a strength and a weakness in Anglicanism. It can be strong, as it was intended to be by the formulations of those Thirty-nine Articles, in 'edifying' and building up the Church. Yet that same comprehensiveness can also feed division and schism within such a broad-beamed Church. What is quite clear is that the kind of imperialistic calling upon power (secular or ecclesiastical) to repress different viewpoints really does not edify the Church. In that respect, Laud was behaving in a very un-Anglican way and it neither helped him nor his Church: he was soon (1641) to leave Lambeth Palace to reside temporarily in the Tower of London (only eight years after his disastrous journey across the Thames to Lambeth) and four years later he was beheaded on Tower Hill where he displayed great serenity and courage.

The comprehensiveness of Anglicanism

Mentally our mind's eye now goes back further still. Buried in Lambeth Palace, underneath the chapel, are the remains of Archbishop Matthew Parker — Queen Elizabeth I's first choice for Archbishop of Canterbury in 1559. Fondly known as 'Nosey Parker' (his portrait hangs in Lambeth Palace) he was very much the moderate man — ideally chosen to hold the central position of the *Ecclesia Anglicana* which Elizabeth I was compelled to orchestrate with moderation as much for political and international reasons as for reasons theological. The brief reign of Queen Mary (Bloody Mary, 1553-1558) had again opened the doors of England to papal intervention and had given to the Pope precisely the jurisdiction in England that Henry VIII and Edward VI, in the first half of the century, had been at such pains to withhold. The Reformation in all its excesses raged in Europe throughout the whole of the sixteenth century and swung violently towards the excesses of Protestantism. It abolished bishops and priests, dethroned the Pope and enthroned the Bible. It threw away with the medieval excesses a superstitious priest-craft, but also many of the valuable practices, doctrines and spiritual insights of the Western Catholic Church.

Happily the Church in England was more modest in its reforms. It was inevitably buffeted by these same European storms, but refused to cut loose from the anchor of apostolic church order, especially in the person of the bishop, or from the catholic expressions of liturgy in the sacraments of the Church. It gave a new prominence to preaching, it insisted upon the use of the vernacular both in the Bible and in the Prayer Book and it permitted its ordained clergy to marry. So we can see now, in our mind's eye, 'Nosey' Parker and Mrs Parker residing openly as man and wife at Lambeth in the 1580's. History tells us that they began to provide for clergy and laity a series of splendid banquets at Lambeth Palace. Queen Elizabeth herself came to visit Archbishop Parker at Canterbury and gave to her loyal and able new Archbishop a massive gold salt cellar valued at two hundred marks to adorn his table and doubtless to impress his manifold guests. It was on this unprecedented occasion that Elizabeth the Queen addressed the wife of the Archbishop with these carefully chosen words: 'Madam I may not call you; mistress I am ashamed to call you, so I know not what to call you; but yet I thank you.'[14]

Matthew Parker, aided later by Richard Hooker, proved to be an excellent chief architect for establishing the foundations of the *Ecclesia Anglicana*. The twenty years prior to Elizabeth's reign had been stormy indeed with a swing first to the left and then to the right; first to Protestant emphases under Edward VI and then back to Roman Catholic extremes under Bloody Mary. Elizabeth was anxious to establish the realm and its religion. Although on the one hand Rome and its Spanish ally must not be offended, on the other hand neither must Protestantism and its French ally be alienated. Elizabeth, like Agag in the Old Testament, had to learn to tread delicately and to steer something of a middle course. For eleven years she kept the Pope sufficiently happy that he did not in fact excommunicate her until 1570. During those years, she established the Church of England in such a way that it retained all its continuity both with the immediate past of Mary and Cardinal Pole, while reforming it with the best insights of the theology and spirituality that had come out of the European Reformation. Furthermore, she created with the help of Matthew Parker a package deal: the Act of Uniformity of 1559 summoned every loyal Englishman to express his loyalties to the Queen by his commitment to the English Church expressed in the English Prayer Book — Cranmer's 1552 *Book of Common Prayer* — with a few modest modifications.

Therefore the unity of the Church of England was never based upon a confession or theological constitution as was the case with so many of the Reformed Churches in the Europe of Elizabeth's day. Rather, it was a living unity and fellowship, and freed from interference from Rome, both political and ecclesiastical, tied to a national loyalty. It was a unity and fellowship focused in the episcopate with the sacraments as the visible signs of that unity. The bishops in their turn swore loyalty to the Monarch as Supreme Governor of the Church. Finally, this unity did not seek to trim the hedges of doctrine with theological nail scissors, but preferred to use the Prayer Book and to see in worship the expression of belief tested pragmatically through prayer, church order and Christian discipleship in everyday life. It was left to Richard Hooker and subsequent Anglican divines to work out a theological mandate for the *Ecclesia Anglicana* as it had emerged in practice rather pragmatically by the close of Elizabeth's long and glorious reign in the year 1603.

That Book of Common Prayer!

So, inevitably, the scene in our mind's eye must now change as we go back even further to the formidable scholar and liturgist, Thomas Cranmer. Enthroned at Canterbury on December the 3rd, 1533, Cranmer had walked barefoot through the cold and sanded streets to sit in the Chair of Augustine[15] — an estimable practice, which might perhaps be reconsidered in our own day! In the two Books of Common Prayer for which he was almost totally and personally responsible (1549 and 1552) he expressed through the worship, the rubrics and the ordinal the essential flexibility of Anglicanism. There are throughout deliberate ambiguities. On the one hand they hold in tension both the claims of catholicism within the Church of England as the English Church had received and experienced that catholicism over the centuries. Those catholic claims focused essentially on the sacramental person of the bishop and those delegated by him to preach the word of God and to administer the sacraments of Christ's catholic Church. On the other hand, those same Prayer Books of Cranmer reflected the best and most moderate insights of contemporary continental Protestantism. They contained a healthy emphasis upon the preaching and teaching of the scriptures, the role of the laity and the use of the vernacular in worship and liturgy. So it was that those with catholic or protestant leanings could alike turn to the same pages of the same Prayer Book (as it was finally compiled in 1662) to vindicate their position within Anglicanism. In fact, between 1549 and 1662 the *Ecclesia Anglicana* was to oscillate between the extremes of catholicism on the one hand and the extremes of protestantism on the other. Both parties alike however saw in the Act of Uniformity and its accompanying Prayer Book the necessary latitude to follow their particular persuasions. Frankly, in that hundred and fifty years or so, so much blood was shed in the name of Christianity and in establishing the *Ecclesia Anglicana* that, with the settlement of 1662 and the Restoration of Charles II, broad churchmen would in future be in favour.

The latitude that is latent in Anglicanism is openly spread across the pages of the history of the Church of England. It is part of the English story and therefore inevitably part of the early chapters of Anglicanism. It probably frustrated and disappointed extremists at either end, while tugging from both directions those who saw the need to hold some middle ground. Yet was it not singularly fitting that in 1956, on the occasion of the four hundredth anniversary of the burning of Thomas Cranmer, Archbishop Geoffrey Fisher, in many ways that most anglican of Anglicans, should move the following resolution at a Convocation of the Church of England:

> 'That this Convocation do now proceed to the Chapel of Lambeth Palace, there to remember before God Thomas Cranmer, Archbishop and Martyr, with thanksgiving for all he restored and gave to the life and worship of the Catholic and Apostolic Church of this land to be our possession and the possession of the whole Anglican Communion throughout the world.'[16]

Some might say, somewhat cynically, that it was a strange gift with mixed blessings. What is certainly true is that we are still working out the implications of the mixture.

Back to the roots of it all

Now our mind's eye must finally leave Lambeth Palace and take the ancient Roman road southeast from London. We are following the road to Canterbury pursued by so many pilgrims over the centuries. Yes — 'in our end is our beginning'.

When Dr Robert Runcie was enthroned as Archbishop of Canterbury in 1980 he swore, as his predecessors had done, to preserve the rites of 'this cathedral and metropolitan Church of Christ, Canterbury'. He took that oath on a book of the Gospels sent to England, so tradition asserts, as early as 601 A.D. Only four years earlier the timid and diffident Benedictine monk, Augustine, together with a party of about forty others, set out from Rome. Bede, in his *Ecclesiastical History of the English People*, tells us how they panicked on that missionary journey and 'paralysed with terror . . . began to contemplate returning home rather than going to a barbarous, fierce and unbelieving nation whose language they did not even understand.'[17] Finally, recovering their nerve and goaded on afresh by Pope Gregory who had sent them in the first place, they reached the channel coast and sailed northwards to the old Roman fort at Dover, into the mouth of the River Stour. At that point they were now only some twelve miles or so from the Roman town of Durovernum (modern Canterbury). The site was as key and strategic as it had been for Julius Caesar when he came to Britain over five centuries earlier.

Augustine was warmly welcomed by the King of East Kent, Aethelbert, and his wife, Bertha, the Christian daughter of Charibert, the Frankish King of Paris. The king and queen travelled from their capital city to meet Augustine and his party. Augustine, through an interpreter, explained the reasons which had brought him, his monks and others to the shores of Kent. He was bearing a silver cross and a picture of the crucifixion, we are told, and came walking in procession and singing a litany, a scene which powerfully evokes the sense of the apostolic nature of the Church of God on the move throughout history. After Augustine had spoken, the king replied: 'We do not wish to do you harm; on the contrary, we will receive you hospitably and provide what is necessary for your support; nor do we forbid you to win all you can to your faith and religion by your preaching.'[18] We are told that some ten thousand people were baptized on Christmas day 597 A.D. and furthermore the king himself went down into the waters of baptism, thus joining his wife who had for some time held the faith of Christ.

For there was already in England a Christian Church. We know that as early as 314 A.D. the Church in Britain was strong enough to send three bishops (from London and possibly from York and Lincoln) to the Council of Arles, and a further three bishops to the Council of Ariminum in 359 A.D. (We are told that they were too poor to be able to afford their own travelling expenses.) Yet the Christianity Augustine found in Britain differed in many details from the customs of the Church he had left behind in Rome. What was he to do? Was he to impose in every detail the rites and ceremonies of the Roman Church? He sought the advice of Pope Gregory. 'The temples of the idols among that people,' wrote the wise Gregory to Augustine, 'should on no account be destroyed . . . It is a good idea to detach them from the service of the devil, and dedicate them to the service of the true God.'[19] For Augustine was genuinely perplexed by what he had found of Christianity in Britain where he discovered a variety of liturgical forms and customs.

'Since we hold the same faith, why do customs vary in different churches, why does the method of saying mass differ in the holy Roman Church and in the Churches of Gaul?'[20]

Why? Because, the Church at its best must always hold a tension between what is local and indigenous and what is universal and catholic; it was that other Augustine (of Hippo) whose mother received the wise advice about rites and ceremonies from the equally wise Bishop of Milan in the dictum which is still well-known to this day: 'When in Rome, do as the Romans do.' *Mutatis mutandis* surely the dictum applies, when in Milan, or Hippo, or Buenos Aires, or Canterbury, or Umpala, do as they do — in secondary matters such as rites and ceremonies. (Echoes of Article XXXIV all over again, perhaps?)

The challenge today

Now we can begin to see how if we allow our minds to range historically, chronologically and geographically over the tree of Anglicanism as we see it today, evolving as it has over the centuries from the acorn of Augustine through its roots in Anglo-Saxon history and Reformation turbulence, we observe branches today spreading in all directions; branches in which the birds of the nations may build their nests — yet nests fabricated and made from what is local and available while resting in the ample accommodation of what is historical, traditional and tested by the winds of history and the storms of controversy.

For Anglicanism rightly prides itself on its comprehensiveness. At its best that is a comprehensiveness for the sake of truth, and not (as so many critics of Anglicanism would like to tell us) a compromise for the sake of peace. Christianity, because it is not an idea or ideology, but is embodied in the lives of people and in the history of nations, has always expanded and extended its branches along the lines of empires and national growth. It was true in the first centuries of Christianity with the roads, the culture, the laws and language of the Roman empire. Necessarily such a Christianity takes to itself some characteristics of that empire and identifies with its culture. But empires come and empires go. The Church of God is destined by the promise of Christ and by the covenant of his Spirit to continue evolving until the close of the age. There is always a danger, as there was when the kingdom of Kent became Christian in the person of its king at his baptism in 597 A.D., that the faith begins to dance to the rhythm of the state instead of the state dancing to the rhythm of Christianity. In reality it should indeed be a dance, yet we need to remember that it takes two to tango theologically: culture *and* faith, state *and* Church.

Some developing tensions

In the nineteenth century, Anglicanism rode on the back of the British Empire in its remarkable expansion throughout the world — and was none the worse for that. Anglicanism is strongly coloured and flavoured with all that is English. It is none the worse for that either. But there also comes a moment when, with the decline of that Empire, Anglicanism needs to adapt its chemistry partly in continuity and partly in discontinuity with its past. Different Churches within different colourings of the Anglican spectrum will explore, develop and evolve as only organic matter can. So, even in nineteenth century English history we see the development of differing emphases within the Church of England.

Evangelicals led the way at the beginning of the nineteenth century, closely followed by the Tractarians and Anglo-Catholics of the later decades. Both saw their roots in the same Church — the latitudinarian church of the previous century — and both claimed to be loyal to the roots of Anglicanism as found in the *Book of Common Prayer* and indeed in the *Ecclesia Anglicana* stretching back to the time of Augustine. Both, in their turn, exported those emphases through various missionary societies with varying colourings and differing rites and ceremonies. At the same time many, like Archbishop Tait, saw the need to hold more closely to the middle ground, tracing their roots through latitudinarianism and broad churchmanship, which had together characterized Anglicanism in the seventeenth century. Yet all in their turn saw the mandate for their position in the same Prayer Book of 1662, in the witness of Elizabeth, in the writings of Cranmer, the balance of Matthew Parker and the theological mandate of Richard Hooker.

Viewed in one way, it has to be admitted that much that we today call Anglicanism is something of an historical accident, yet the same picture catching a slightly different angle of light can equally bear a rather less cynical interpretation. For while retaining a healthy cynicism (or perhaps humour would be a better word) we can also discern something of the hand of God in all of this.

In vesture, gesture, and posture, there are many (and for some) alarming differences of emphasis and attitude in contemporary Anglican practice. Furthermore, there is a tendency to form within contemporary Anglicanism parties – and eventually (if left to go their own way) the temptation to unchurch opposing parties and differing emphases. But we do need to ask again and again: 'Where are the edges to this great comprehensive Church?' Surely it is much healthier not to be too concerned with drawing lines at the edges for the sake of exclusion and tidiness. A vacuum, it is true, is always concerned to bolster up its edges: a vacuum is defined by what it keeps out, and is designed to resist *im*plosions from the outside. On the other hand, life – developing life, like the universe – is much more of an *ex*plosion. The extent of an explosion is perhaps best defined (if it is defined at all) by its strength at the centre. It was Bishop John Robinson who defined a radical as someone who was so strong and secure at the centre that he could afford to go to the edges. More important, it was Jesus of Nazareth who said that in his mission those who were not against him were for him. (Luke 9:50)

The place of places

It is perhaps significant that most Lambeth Conferences (except some of the early ones) have found it necessary and compelling to take at some point in their deliberations a pilgrimage to some place on English soil which reflected the many faces of Anglicanism in all its diversity throughout the centuries.

The Conference of 1897, to celebrate the thirteen hundredth centenary of Augustine's arrival in England, invited the Lambeth Fathers to visit Ebbsfleet. Nearby Canterbury is of course heavy with the history not only of Augustine but also with the lives of other architects of the *Ecclesia Anglicana* – Anselm, Lanfranc and Thomas Becket. Frequently over the years the bishops have visited the great centres of northern Anglicanism — for example Durham, with its honoured associations with St Cuthbert, John Cosin and Joseph Butler. In 1908 they undertook a somewhat disastrous pilgrimage to Lindisfarne. We are told that on that occasion, several of the ladies 'accompanying them fell from their carriages into the water'. Over the years Lambeth has in wonderful ways sought to explore the diversity and extension of its Anglican roots during the course of its Conferences, with visits to Lincoln, where the memory and spirit of Robert Grosseteste, St Hugh and Edward King are vividly recalled; Bath and Wells in the 1878 Conference for the memento of Bishop Thomas Ken. The tapestry is huge and the faces and features of Anglicanism manifold. There is St Chad of Litchfield, John Colet and John Donne of St Paul's. Then there are Ridley, Latimer and Cranmer at Oxford. In 1897 a solemn pilgrimage was led by the ageing Archbishop Frederick Temple to Glastonbury, the shrine of pre-Augustinian Christianity. The English climate on that occasion was so uncharacteristically sunny and hot that many thought the successor of St Augustine would faint in the heat![21]

Yet having said all this (and much that has been left unsaid) it has to be admitted that today Anglicanism is diversifying in ways that many find not only exciting but terrifying. In the past we have often unchurched Anglicans who appeared to want to pull the Communion away from its centre, rooted as it should be in scripture, tradition and reason. Wesley in the seventeenth century went too far in one direction. Cardinal Newman in the nineteenth century went too far in the opposite direction, while F.D. Maurice was never comfortable in the Church of England and found its tensions somewhat inhospitable. Christian witness and life are only possible if we are centred and anchored (perhaps life in any form is only possible when it is in touch with its own centre). Heresy is literally a question of being out of touch, running amok, first in this direction and then in that. Accordingly, the question still needs to be asked and was asked again at Lambeth in 1988 with some passion: what is the heart and centre of Anglicanism? Without a 'constitution' or 'confession', what will keep Anglicans together at the centre, while permitting them also to extend at the edges, interpenetrating varieties of culture and clothing the Gospel in the colour and vesture of new ages and different languages?

The 'quadrilateral' of Anglicanism

The Episcopal Church in America in its General Convention in Chicago in 1886 drew up a document of four principles within which the unity and integrity of Anglicanism could be maintained and further shared with other Christian Churches in all discussions about authority, pluralism, diversity and unity. In the Lambeth Conference of 1888, under the leadership of Archbishop Benson, the bishops reiterated the statement which had come out of Chicago only two years earlier. They tidied it up and produced it in a form which has come to be known as the Lambeth Quadrilateral (though perhaps it would be more appropriate and accurate to call it, as some do, the Chicago-Lambeth Quadrilateral).

It read as follows:

'In the opinion of this Conference, the following articles supply a basis on which approach may be, by God's blessing, made towards Home Reunion.

a) The Holy Scriptures of the Old and New Testaments, as "containing all things necessary to salvation", and as being the rule and ultimate standard of faith.

b) The Apostles' Creed, as the Baptismal Symbol; and the Nicene Creed, as the sufficient statement of the Christian faith.

c) The two Sacraments ordained by Christ Himself — Baptism and the Supper of the Lord — ministered with unfailing use of Christ's words of Institution, and of the elements ordained by Him.

d) The Historic Episcopate, locally adapted in the methods of its administration to the varying needs of the nations and peoples called by God into the Unity of His Church.'[22]

There it is: Scriptures, Creeds, Sacraments, Historic Episcopate. It is a quadrilateral. Whatever else may be in the casserole, these four basic ingredients ensure an Anglican recipe. On the lips of Archbishop Benson, in 1888, Resolution XI seemed perhaps to put the matter finally to rest.

But no. The scene has changed yet again. In 1930 the ghosts of Lambeth are still discussing the issues and questions of 1888. These incidentally are the same questions asked in 1988! We can be forgiven for asking if Lambeth Conferences have ever solved anything? 'Nothing is settled' wrote the angry Suffragan Bishop of Peterborough in 1897, after the Lambeth Conference of the same year. 'No perplexing problem is solved, no burning questions bravely grappled with.'[23]

Faced with the daunting questions raised by the Church of South India scheme for reunion (which was to haunt several Lambeth Conferences) Archbishop Lang had approached the 1930 Conference very apprehensively. He was not in good health and somewhat dreaded further extended discussions on the vexing questions of unity and therefore on the further questions of the spirit of Anglicanism. What can and cannot be in union with a Church which is itself notoriously unclear about the nature of its own unity? Resolution XXXXIX ('a subject of portentous dullness'[24] according to one bishop present), rang around the walls of Juxon's Hall, Lambeth. In the collegiality of the ages, is it too foolish to wonder what the ghosts of Augustine, Becket, Cranmer, Parker, Laud and a whole invisible communion that no man could number, felt as the words of yet another Resolution went on and on . . . on and on?

'The Conference approves the following statement of the nature and status of the Anglican Communion . . . .The Anglican Communion is a fellowship, within the One, Holy Catholic and Apostolic Church, of those duly constituted Dioceses, Provinces or Regional Churches in communion with the See of Canterbury, which have the following characteristics in common:

a) they uphold and propagate the Catholic and Apostolic faith and order as they are generally set forth in the *Book of Common Prayer* as authorised in their several churches [Can we see Cranmer smiling, perhaps somewhat smugly?]

b) they are particular or national Churches, and, as such, promote within each of their territories a national expression of Christian faith, life and worship; [perhaps the ghost of Laud is looking irritated and somewhat apprehensive], and

c) they are bound together not by a central legislative and executive authority, but by mutual loyalty sustained through the common counsel of the Bishops in conference.'[25] [Is that Archbishop Longley nodding approvingly though perhaps with Bishop Gray and Bishop Colenso in opposite corners of the hall remaining somewhat cynical?]

'The Conference makes this statement,' continued Archbishop Lang in somewhat imperialistic tones,

'praying for and eagerly awaiting the time when the Churches of the present Anglican Communion will enter into communion with other parts of the Catholic Church not definable as Anglican in the above sense, as a step towards the ultimate reunion of all Christendom in one visibly united fellowship.'[26]

(We could perhaps be forgiven for assuming that every Lambeth Conference says the same thing in a slightly different key, every ten years.)

Still seeking unity?

The scene has changed, yet again, but this time for the last time. We are back where we began. A silence has settled over the assembled bishops in the gymnasium of Kent University. The one hundred and second successor to Augustine picks up his papers and prepares to address the twelfth Lambeth Conference. The topic? Exactly one hundred years after the confident Resolution XI of the 1888 Conference, the Archbishop of Canterbury, the Most Reverend and Right Honourable Robert Runcie, Primate of All England presiding over the twelfth Lambeth Conference prepares to speak and the title, as we have seen, is somewhat inevitably: 'The Nature of the Unity We Seek . . . .'

However, we need not be too cynical if the question he is tackling appears to us to be such a hardy annual. In many ways it is the question not only for all Christians throughout the ages since the time of the first apostles (though it is just that and we do well to remind ourselves of that truth). Some Churches at some points in history might pretend that they have found the answer to this vexed question of unity in forms of church government and hierarchical authority. Nevertheless, again and again, like Archbishop Laud and many through the ages, they have had to summon powerful political sanctions of a nature not unlike that of the medieval inquisition to uphold their views of such a static form of unity. (The successors of St Peter have frequently picked up the sword of secular power to defend the Body of Christ — the very sword that Christ specifically asked Peter to put away in the garden of His sufferings.)

For this question of unity is not only a question for the Church. It is the question of the ages and of the nations. 'The unity we seek' which will give both individual and corporate freedom and which will permit rich and diverse growth — that unity has so far eluded fallen humanity. The prayer of Jesus that we might be one was modelled on nothing less than an icon of the unity which he shares with his Father in the fellowship of the Holy Spirit, which is the Trinity, unscarred by sin. While we must work and pray in every generation for that unity, as we pray for the Kingdom, it is something we shall never orchestrate nor establish on this planet. In the meantime there has necessarily to be a strong sense of living provisionally. At its best, the whole vocation of Anglicanism is provisional. On an earlier occasion, Archbishop Runcie was adamant. 'It is important,' he said, 'that we never permanently canonize Anglicanism. Denominations — including our own Anglican Communion — are only provisional necessities because of the frailty of human nature and the failure of Christian charity.'[27] In a body or organism unity is health. In a nation it is peace. In the Church it is nothing less than a charism of love — that love of which St Paul sings in such lyrical and poetical tones in the thirteenth chapter of his first Epistle to the Corinthians. In this world such unity is seldom glimpsed. In heaven it is the constant vision of the saints in that eternal sabbath; it is the shalom and peace experienced only in worship and adoration.

In 1936, the late Bishop Ramsey wrote these words. They are words which perhaps say it all, while in no way diminishing the necessity for a continuing struggle to become the sort of Church for which Jesus prayed — a Church in which we would all be one as He is one with His Father.

'For while the Anglican Church is vindicated by its place in history, with a strikingly balanced witness to Gospel and Church and sound learning, its greater vindication lies in pointing through its own history to something of which it is a fragment. Its credentials are its incompleteness with the tension and the travail in its soul. It is clumsy and untidy, it baffles neatness and logic. For it is sent not to commend itself as "the best type of Christianity", but by its very brokenness to point to the universal Church wherein all have died.'[28]

REFERENCES

[1] Bishop Adrián Cáceres, *Crossroads Are for Meeting,* S.P.C.K., 1986, p. 283

[2] Edward Carpenter, *Cantuar: The Archbishops in Their Office,* Cassell, London, 1971, p. 335

[3] R.T. Davidson, *Life of Archibald Campbell Tait, Archbishop of Canterbury,* Macmillan & Co., London, 1891, Vol. II, p. 268.

[4] Edward Carpenter, *Cantuar: The Archbishops in Their Office,* Cassell, London, 1971, p. 333

[5] Ibid., p. 328

[6] Alan M.G. Stephenson, *Anglicanism and the Lambeth Conferences,* S.P.C.K., London, 1978, p. 36

[7] Ibid., p. 37

[8] Edward Carpenter, *Cantuar: The Archbishops in Their Office,* Cassell, London, 1971, p. 330

[9] Ibid.

[10] Ibid.

[11] John Howe, *Highways and Hedges, Anglicanism and the Universal Church,* Anglican Book Centre, Toronto, Ontario, 1985, p. 79

[12] Edward Carpenter, *Cantuar: The Archbishops in Their Office,* Cassell, London, 1971, p. 190

[13] Ibid., p. 193

[14] Ibid., p. 151

[15] Ibid., p. 135

[16] Ibid., p 142

[17] Ibid., p. 3

[18] Ibid., p. 4

[19] Bede, *A History of The English Church and People, Book I,* Chapter 30, Penguin, 1968

[20] Ibid.

[21] Alan M.G. Stephenson, *Anglicanism and the Lambeth Conferences,* S.P.C.K., London, 1978, p. 4

[22] Ibid., p. 5 ff

[23] Ibid., p. 104

[24] Ibid., p 172

[25] *The Lambeth Conferences,* S.P.C.K., London 1948, p 173 ff

[26] Ibid., p. 174

[27] Archbishop Runcie, Lecture II: 'The Anglican Response', Trinity Institute, New York, 1988

[28] A.M. Ramsey, *The Gospel and the Catholic Church,* Longmans, 1936, p. 220

CHAPTER THREE

Controversy, Conflict and
Communion

*'The Church has to understand, describe and live its unity without
destroying the gifts of diversity on the one hand or being broken apart by
the tensions of its diversity on the other.'[1]*

Canon Samuel Van Culin

Conflict

'It is, I believe, one of the chief weaknesses of the documents of the
Second Vatican Council,' wrote Stephen Sykes, 'that it conspicuously
fails to expect conflict in the Church.'[2] Yet, since the earliest days of
the Church, in the New Testament and continuously ever since, the
Church has been in conflict. It is the nature of the beast! In fact one
could go further and say that it is often when the Church has been at
its liveliest that it has been most in conflict. Neither should that surprise us. Passion and platitudes seldom sit well together; and there are
few places more peaceful, hushed and silent than a graveyard! (The
Psalmist makes the point eloquently: 'The dead do not praise the
Lord!' A praising Church is a living Church, and a living Church can
be all too painfully alive at times — just like the Corinthian Church of
St Paul's day.) Wherever men and women in Church or state have
cared passionately and come alive for the truth's sake, there has been
conflict. Conflict and tension lie at the very heart of life and there will
always be plenty of it at the heart of a living and lively Church.

Nevertheless, it has to be said that the Anglican Communion in the
last decades of the twentieth century is experiencing perhaps more
than its fair share of conflict and controversy. 'These are critical times
for Anglicanism.'[3] As we have seen, the first Lambeth Conference

was convened with conflict and tension hidden on the agenda (the Colenso affair). Successive Lambeth Conferences have had their fair share of passionate debate, controversy and conflict. However, the 1980's have proved to be stormy waters indeed for the Anglican Communion with debates at every level in the life of our Church — debates which have raised passions, pumping out reports and counter-reports on an unprecedented scale.

To the sceptic or outside observer, much of this must appear as little better than internal ecclesiastical squabbling, a sort of twentieth century version of the ultimately absurd medieval debating caricature concerning the number of angels that can dance on the point of a needle.

Writing of the Church of England (and much the same can be said of whole parts of the Anglican Communion today) one writer tells us that it all 'resembles a man who has bought a motorcar for the purpose of seeing the countryside.' However, he 'has become so fascinated with his purchase that he spends Saturdays and Sundays tinkering with the engine rather than speeding over the Downs.' He goes on: 'So, at any rate, to those who are not church hobbyists, do many current ecclesiastical debates appear: no more so than the faintly ludicrous question of whether women should be ordained to the priesthood.'[4] Such has always been a problem for the Church in its institutional form — namely, that 'like most organizations' it would appear 'more concerned with its own internal workings than with the function which it is presumably meant to fulfil.'[5]

Synods — whether deanery, diocesan or provincial (to say nothing of the Anglican Consultative Council or Lambeth Conferences) — will begin to take up more and more time, money and energy. The price of consultation nearly always results in a slower pace and a larger bill. Furthermore, it is not long before means become ends, priorities become confused and what is really 'as of first importance' is lost in the in-tray marked 'urgent' of the bureaucrat. Are expensive meetings such as Lambeth really to be spent on apparently trivial questions of ecclesiastical ordering and machinery? Certainly in the Church of England and the Episcopal Church in the United States of America in the decades since the Second World War, an inordinate amount of time, money, paper and talk have been devoted to issues which (at least at first sight) would appear to be the concerns of 'church hobbyists': new liturgy and new prayer books, women priests (and now bishops):

endless debates over inclusive God language and the ordination of homosexuals whether male or female. In fairness it has to be said that this is more the impression gained from a first, quick glance primarily perhaps through the perspective of the media. The facts are however more impressive on closer inspection.

The General Synod of the Church of England has mounted debates of exceptionally high calibre on matters which are of the greatest possible concern to our world and to society. The debates on racism and the report of the General Synod, *Faith in the City*, spoke eloquently in the name of the Gospel. History will probably show how such debates effected even government policy across the road in the halls of Westminster. It was that articulate guru of the London *Times,* Bernard Levin, who emerged staggering from the debate of the General Synod of the Church of England on homosexuality. After his usual somewhat acidic remarks, he nevertheless felt compelled to conclude:

> 'I emerged with a wondering but intense admiration for this amazing body. The Church of England, facing for once a real problem, predictably and inevitably fudged it. But in the very act of fudging, it spoke with tongues. It will be denounced from within and without its ranks, for both cowardice and brutality; but the result was a victory for all the best qualities of this country. The Church is as puzzled, worried and uncertain as the rest of us; but in a strange way, it gave us all a lead, if only by telling us that to be puzzled, worried and uncertain is the lot of all thinking people, and it is no shame to confess as much.'[6]

Conflict and change

Surely that is so — for what are the alternatives? Fundamentalism? Ecclesiastical totalitarianism? Self-styled infallibility? Easy answers to difficult questions? Surely we can learn from history. Whenever the Church has gone in feet-first with slick, trim and easy answers, it has nearly always been proved, in the long run, to be in the wrong. The Church is not exempt from the headaches and the heartaches which are common in the society and world which the Church seeks to serve in the name of Jesus Christ. Conflict, controversy and tension will be its lot, till the end of time. That is the bad news. The good news is that the Christian Church differs from the world precisely insofar as it can be gifted by the Holy Spirit of God himself, who will be with us in those heartaches and yearnings till the end of time. The promise was to lead us into all truth, but not all in the first five minutes!

For the genius and contribution of Anglicanism lies in its very willingness to suffer and be patient for the truth's sake. Of course it all sounds very wonderful, and pretty grand, but the thorny question which is burgeoning increasingly in Anglicanism in our day is quite simply: does it work and will it work? While Anglicanism was to all intents and purposes the same as the nation of England at prayer (until the eighteenth century) the experiment worked well. That Church was answerable to Parliament, whose leaders were of course members of the Church of England to a man. They were almost exclusively from the same public schools, universities (Oxford and Cambridge) and members of the same London clubs. The leaders of the Church all came from the same stable, married into the same families and drank at the same bars. The unity of such a Church, therefore, was primarily social and only secondly theological.

Indeed the first nine Lambeth Conferences were chaired by Archbishops of Canterbury who had all been headmasters (with only two exceptions, Cosmo Gordon Lang and Randall Davidson) of major public schools. Randall Davidson was nevertheless grafted into this strange family tree by his marriage to the second daughter of a former Archbishop (Tait). The tenth Lambeth Conference was chaired by an Archbishop (Ramsey) who was a pupil at the school where the previous Archbishop, Fisher, had been headmaster. These archiepiscopal peas are all from the same cultural pod.

Little wonder that Archbishop Longley might be forgiven for dealing with the Colenso controversy in much the same way as he had dealt with controversies and difficulties in the senior common room of Harrow. After all, Colenso had been the maths master at that very school. For Anglicanism, like all of Christianity, has its origins in a tightly homogeneous culture, and need not necessarily be any the worse for that. Yet if its stays there, it decays there.

Much of this has changed of course, and changed rapidly in the one hundred and twenty years since the first Lambeth Conference of

1867. Most Englishmen are no longer practising Anglicans and most Anglicans in the world are no longer Englishmen. The climate, culture and environment in which Anglicanism is growing today are all very different from the world in which Cranmer protested, Laud was arrested or Longley suggested the first Lambeth Conference. Furthermore, not only are most Anglicans in the world no longer Englishmen, but they are no longer either members of the British Empire or the British Commonwealth. It is truly difficult to know any longer in what real sense Anglicans are anglicans — if by that word you mean something remotely connected with England. Anglicanism has to confess to having something of an identity crisis.

So Archbishop Runcie puts the question: 'Some of us need to ask whether we have confined the Risen Christ and seen him only in Western cultural dress.'[7] Yet it was Archbishop Geoffrey Fisher (himself the archetype of that long succession of headmasters from leading public schools) who was, as we have seen, perhaps the most instrumental of all Archbishops of Canterbury up to his day in breaking out of the mould of the Church of England and releasing Anglicanism upon a variety of cultures. Ironically, it was a headmaster from Repton School who gave to Anglicanism its first chapter of independence, autonomy and a strong encouragement towards raising up an indigenous ministry. That has to be the work of grace! Although Anglicanism still has a long way to go in evolving a truly intercultural and international order, it has nevertheless set its face firmly and resolutely in that direction and is now beginning to face some of the conflicts and pains of those decisions taken so swiftly and resolutely by that irascible headmaster immediately after the Second World War. Having put the cat of imperialism firmly out through the back window in the 'fifties, the tiger of pluralism and independence is firmly stamping up to the front door of Lambeth in the 'eighties.

For most of the conflict, tension and questions in Anglicanism today arise from two sources, both of which are proudly the strength of the Anglican way of doing things. The first of these is the result of this explosion of Christianity out of the mould of one particular culture, in time and space, into a variety of cultures. Yet if Anglicanism is to fly, it must leave the nest and cradle of its origins. So there will be some who would question even the title 'Anglican', fearing it to be too constricting, limiting and backward looking. (Archbishop Fisher, of all people, did precisely that while addressing the General Convention of the Episcopal Church as long ago as 1946.)

Yet by the principle of the Incarnation, God is necessarily 'down-to-earth'. So with the Church. It is not ashamed to be dressed and to express itself in the local cultural clothing of its day — with all the dangers inherent in that kind of tailoring.

'The idea that one can or could at any time separate out by some process of distillation a pure Gospel unadulterated by any cultural accretions is an illusion. It is, in fact, an abandonment of the Gospel, for the Gospel is about the word made flesh. Every statement of the Gospel in words is conditioned by the culture of which those words are a part, and every style of life that claims to embody the truth of the Gospel is a culturally conditioned style of life. There can never be a culture-free Gospel.'[8]

The same is true when we begin to discuss a Christianity which has expressed itself largely through nations and empires. That somewhat eccentric Anglican, Dr Alec Vidler, reminded Anglicans long ago that,

'No one will be able to understand . . . the English Church and the Anglican Communion, who supposes that the Catholic Church and National Churches are incompatible, or that as a Church becomes more Catholic, it becomes less national, or who doubts that the Kingdom of Christ consecrates the life of nations . . . . [The existence of the Anglican Communion] is a living protest on behalf of the principle of nationality, and of the direct responsibility of bishops and rulers to Christ, and against the notion of a visible head of the Church and a centralized (Church) government.'[9]

So Anglicanism will always continue to wear something of the remnant (albeit perhaps only underclothing) of Henry VIII, Augustine of Canterbury, Abbess Hilda of Whitby, the Mother of Parliaments, Oxford and Cambridge, English public schools and perhaps that most English of all characteristics — the gift for permanent and considerable understatement. Yet, as Anglicanism evolves, it will require new styles and different dress, in varying and apparently conflicting colours, ranging from the Indian culture in northern Canada to the tribal cultures of central Africa, to say nothing of the eastern cultures or even the distinctively un-English culture of the United States of America! For the balancing truth to the principle of Incarnation (that Jesus was born at a particular time and in a particular place), which rightly emphasizes the local and temporal, is the principle of the Ascension (that Jesus rose and ascended beyond time and space) which lifts our eyes and demands another emphasis upon the universal, the eternal and the catholic. In this world what is local and indigenous will always be in conflict with what is universal and worldwide.

For example, where in that tension and on that spectrum do we put feminism or homosexual lifestyle? What about those discussions concerning polygamy which were there somewhat in the background at the first Lambeth Conference and which have certainly not gone away? An imperialistic view of mission would quite simply export the Gospel, content and container, as a package deal: take it or leave it. It would seek to know nothing of such conflicts and would be impatient in any protracted discussions on such issues. 'When in Rome do as the Romans do' will not suffice such an impatience: when in Rome, Constantinople, Canterbury, Umpala or Tibet — still do as the Romans do? Such an argument will want nothing to do with the use of the vernacular in worship: Latin (or the Shakespearean Book of Common Prayer) was good enough for our forefathers, it must be good enough for us and it shall be good enough for you!

So if you call together the leaders of a multicoloured and multicultural communion such as the Anglican Communion, without the streamlined advantages of an infallible chairman (or disadvantage, depending on how you see it) you had better be ready for trouble, controversy, disagreement and tension. Yet as we saw in chapter two, Anglicanism has from the outset set its face against the model of Roman Catholicism and has gone for the more subtle and illusive model of unity articulated in that courageous word 'communion'. So, fasten your safety belts, there may be a little turbulence — which is precisely another example of that English characteristic of understatement: in fact, such a road will inevitably be a hell of a rough ride!

What kind of authority?

Behind the discussions about conflicting and alternative cultures, there is in Anglicanism, and especially today, a second, deeper and potentially more explosive question: the question of authority.

'What is at stake for us now is the question of how we are to think about the very nature of the Church, and beyond that, and even more fundamentally, the question of how we are to think about the nature of the faith itself: what we might call the doctrine of Doctrine. What is the Church, and what does it believe? By what authority does it believe it? How does it minister to individual souls, and to human society as a whole? What are and ought to be the effects of the surrounding culture on the actual content of our belief? What is the content of that belief?'[10]

What indeed? More succinctly, though no less urgently:

'Such matters will figure prominently in the forthcoming Lambeth Conference where questions of authority will again be highly prominent.'[11]

Anglicanism has rightly been proud of its comprehensiveness, and its commitment to pluralism. Yet will it prove to be after all just a massive, failed experiment? It would seem that some of those free-range theological and doctrinal chickens so generously let loose throughout Anglican history are now coming home to roost — with the address of Lambeth '88 firmly attached to them. History, in general, would suggest (and post-Vatican II history in particular would loudly proclaim) that it is when you take off the lid of authoritarianism from the kettle of church order that every one rapidly vaporizes into becoming his own pope. Anarchy is not the disappearance of authority but rather the fragmentation of rival and competing authorities. Where you have been compelled to believe everything, the danger will always be not that you revert simply to believing nothing but that on the contrary you compulsively rush out and believe anything. Revolution seldom throws off authoritarianism: it almost always issues in a new tyranny, often the most satanic of all — authoritarianism dressed in the clothes of liberalism. You seldom substitute open-mindedness for authoritarianism. The task is more demanding. You have to find a good doctrinal authority in place of a bad one. It will not be sufficient to say that Anglicanism exists for the sake of what it is not.

That Anglicanism has turned its back on fundamentalism and on ecclesiastical totalitarianism is not enough to rescue it from anarchy. If we are neither biblical fundamentalists in our attitude to scripture, nor ecclesiastical fundamentalists in response to papal authority, then where on earth is the authority of Anglicanism to be found? This is a fundamental question for all Christians as we come to the close of the millenium.

It could be that by the very nature of Anglicanism, Anglicans have been compelled to face this question more obviously and earlier than other Christian traditions. Nor should we be ashamed of spending ink, money, time and energy on the question. For, in many ways, it is the question of our age. The climate of our secular world is strangely such that, in our day, there are very few in the East or the West, rich or poor, of any coloured skin, and of any or no religious affiliation, who do not have a real problem with authority.

Authority and its kindred word, power, are at the heart of all the struggles in our world today. Perhaps it is no bad thing for the Church to put this to the top of its agenda, so that perhaps we may have a freeing word of Gospel and new life for our generation. For society today is torn between tyranny and anarchy; between fundamentalism and liberalism. We see this on every frontier, stretching from the political and sociological with apartheid and terrorism as the most obvious outward signs, all the way across to the moral and ethical frontiers with AIDS and abortion so manifestly in evidence. Have we a truly liberating word to say among all this clamour?

For the ground of this question of authority is shifting rapidly in the 'eighties. The 'fifties and 'sixties witnessed a massive rejection of authority in all its manifestations. That was the age of the crisis of authority. The Left was 'in': politically, ideologically and in every way. However something has happened in recent years. 'To talk about authority in 1988 is more complicated than it was in 1968', said Archbishop Runcie lecturing in New York in 1988 when he pointed to this radical shift. 'The truth is,' he warned us,

> 'the situation which confronts us in 1988 is very different. Now we must speak, not only of the crisis of authority, but also of its comeback. Throughout the world, and in a variety of different cultures, in the Islamic East as well as the Christian West, there is a sharp reassertion of what are held to be "old" values. Economic liberalism seems to be paving the way for moral conservatism and theological liberalism seems to be giving way to unrestricted fundamentalism. The New Right seems here to stay.'[12]

In other words, the *crisis* of authority in the 'sixties has given way to a craving for authority in the 'eighties. A plague on both your houses! Perhaps the close of the twentieth century, at least in the U.K., will parallel the close of the nineteenth century: for Victorianism, now read Thatcherism!

Yes, Archbishop Runcie is surely right. The reactionary reign of Ratzinger and Pope John Paul II may be more 'with it' than against it: more of a response than a reaction. The alternation between liberalism and reaction is recurring in history yet again. For surely it is fear which feeds fundamentalism, and as we come to the end of the millenium, there is much 'fear for what is coming on the earth' (Mark 13). As new waves of fear roar and tides of apprehension break over our planet, we shall all be tempted to look for new golden calves to which we are ready to give unconditional, unquestioning allegiance and worship.

Individualism and interdependence

Yet Archbishop Runcie in that same address was right to go deeper and to ask what other insights will lead us away from the high liberalism of the 'fifties and 'sixties.

> 'We seem to be discovering that individualism is simply not enough. . . . The real world is not like that. So the unquestioning pursuit of the goal of economic liberalism has led to the recent collapse of the money markets and the painful rediscovery of our interdependence – what happens on Wall Street affects what happens on the London market, and what happens in Tokyo affects them both! . . . This interdependence, this inability of any nation to be an island is of course known, and of course much more painfully in the Third World as it struggles with its debts and is forced to conform to the requirements of the IMF.'

'So,' he concludes with resounding affirmation, 'we wake to the truth that interdependence is not the wild ideal of dreamers, but simply the way things are.'[13]

If this is so, economically and politically, it is even more so morally. The brain-washing of the years of liberalism (with the advent of the pill and penicillin) tried to persuade us that sexual morality was purely a matter for the individual conscience, providing 'nobody got hurt'. Two factors in different fields have emerged in the 'eighties which have exploded that little heresy: AIDS and environmental pollution. After all, it would seem, I am my brother's keeper at the end of the day (though perhaps not in the first five minutes as I spread my wings of new-found freedom) and that individualism applied in at least two areas — sexual promiscuity and pollution — will bring a plague to our planet in which millions may well be consumed — many of them 'innocently'. So, in the words of Archbishop Runcie, 'Cooperation should be seen for what it is, an essential part of being human' and morality is after all found to be 'grounded in more than self-interest'.[14]

So in many ways the stage for Lambeth is set not just by ecclesiastical producers and directors, but also by thinking men and women throughout the world. Throughout the history of the Church the finest theology has been developed in response to current events, and indeed Jesus in the New Testament upbraids his hearers for their refusal to read the signs of the times in discerning the Kingdom of God. It was not for nothing that Augustine heatedly reached for his pen in 410 A.D. when the Vandals sacked Rome. In the Fall of Rome, the city of the world had fallen. Was not such a moment a glorious opportunity to point to that other city — 'the City of God'? In the 1930's when German Christians were tailoring and trimming the Gospel of Christ to fit comfortably into the demonic evils of Hitlerism, there was another such opportunity. It was at such a time that Barth pointed with a new insight and urgency to the craggy and robust truth of Revelation — a revelation which would withstand the passing vogues of the age, offering nothing less than redemption, salvation, and grace for the human predicament. So, in an age of neo-fundamentalism, there are fear and the temptation to return to totalitarianism: in such an age, the Church has both the opportunity and the responsibility to seek to discern 'a yet more excellent way'. At its best, Anglicanism could prove equal to such a challenge.

Authority in Anglicanism

Interestingly enough, it was an earlier Lambeth Conference (1948) which produced a quite magnificent report on the nature of authority in Anglicanism (see p. 15). It was never received as a resolution, yet it is one of the classical statements about authority in Anglicanism and one which all the participants of Lambeth '88 should have received as mandated reading in preparation for the events at Canterbury in 1988. For the questions posed at the 1948 Lambeth Conference are essentially the same questions facing the Anglican Communion in 1988.

> 'Is Anglicanism based on a sufficiently coherent form of authority to form the nucleus of a worldwide fellowship of Churches, or does its comprehensiveness conceal internal divisions which may cause its disruption?'[15]

The question which the Fathers at Lambeth raised in 1948 has not gone away. The issues to which that basic question is addressed only forty years later would astonish those same Fathers of 1948. Archbishop Fisher was certainly far-seeing and did more than most to enable the pluralism of Anglicanism, but it is doubtful whether he could have foreseen the possibility of women bishops in some parts of the Anglican Communion less than half a century later. For the question stands: how comprehensive is comprehensive? Perhaps we shall not know the answer to that question until we first address the more radical and almost perennial question: 'By what authority are you doing these things, and who gave you this authority?' (Matthew 21:23) The report of 1948 confidently responds:

> 'Authority as inherited by the Anglican Communion from the undivided Church of the early centuries of the Christian era, is single in that it is derived from a single divine source, and reflects within itself the richness and historicity of the divine Revelation, the authority of the eternal Father, the incarnate Son, and the life-giving Spirit. It is distributed among Scripture, Tradition, Creeds, the Ministry of the Word and Sacraments, the witness of saints and the *consensus fidelium,* which is the continuing experience of the Holy Spirit through his faithful people in the Church. It is thus a dispersed rather than a centralized authority having many elements which combine, interact with and check each other.'[16]

Yes, it sounds fine. Could such a statement foresee that within just forty years there would be bishops at a Lambeth Conference who would not be willing to address God as 'the eternal Father, the incarnate Son and the life-giving Spirit?' We are told today that such language is sexist and should be changed to God the Creator, Redeemer and Sanctifier. Many would argue that if tradition does not stop at a particular point in Church history, but is a continuing process, can it not develop in ways that would find precedents neither in 'Scripture, Tradition, Creeds, the Ministry of the Word and Sacrament' nor 'the witness of saints'? As Anglicans, surely we have to reply — 'no'. Furthermore, as Anglicans, we would have to reply that such lines of argument are derived neither from Scripture, Tradition nor Reason, and should not therefore be 'required' as necessary to salvation. The problem is no new one. Anglicans faced it at the Reformation in the sixteenth century and they did not respond by saying that anyone could believe anything. With the subjective experience of Anabaptists on the one side and the Thomist traditions of the medieval Church on the other, Anglicans picked out a road which led neither into the ditch nor over the precipice. Furthermore, the developing tradition of Anglicanism requires that all developments in doctrine are tested and eventually owned by the *consensus fidelium* which is the continuing experience of the Holy Spirit working through his faithful people in the Church. So we might ask whether that *consensus fidelium* can be discerned in a national or a provincial synod, a meeting of the Lambeth bishops, the mind of the Primates, the Anglican Consultative Council, or some general ecumenical worldwide synod, which does not exist at the present time and which shows no likelihood of coming into existence. Furthermore, at such gatherings, how do we discern the *consensus fidelium?**

* In his address to Trinity Institute in 1988, Archbishop Runcie offered a wise, subtle, yet profoundly simple paraphrase of *consensus fidelium*: 'I sometimes like to translate it,' he said 'as the common sense of the People of God.'

Decision-making in the Church

Does a straight majority as in parliamentary democracy carry the day? Are there winners and losers? Does a narrow (very narrow) majority of the General Convention of the Episcopal Church in the United States on the question of the ordination of women to the priesthood in 1976 constitute a mandate to develop tradition and the practice of the Church in the gift and charism of Holy Orders? Furthermore, does it constitute such a mandate that such beliefs shall be required of all who call themselves Anglicans? Clearly, this is all far from simple. The 1948 Lambeth report goes on to expound on its understanding of dispersed authority.

'Where this authority of Christ is to be found mediated not in one mode but in several, we recognize in this multiplicity God's loving provision against the temptations to tyranny and the dangers of unchecked power.'[17]

The synods of our Church, as well as vestries and church councils at a more local level, need to reconsider their whole process of decision-making. Practice in many of our Churches today points to the apostolic and patient practice of waiting upon the Lord until a common mind emerges. Voting, lobbying, majorities and minorities, should constitute an alien language for the Body of Christ as it seeks the mind of Christ under the Spirit of Christ. The 1948 report continues:

'This authority (dispersed authority) possesses a suppleness and elasticity in that the emphasis of one element over the others may and does change with the changing conditions of the Church. The variety of the contributing factors gives to it a quality of richness which encourages and releases initiative, trains in fellowship and evokes a free and willing obedience.'[18]

Yes, surely that is the goal of true authority — to elicit 'free and willing obedience'.[19] It is the only obedience we see in Jesus in relationship to his Father in the New Testament, and furthermore it is the only obedience he seeks to elicit from others to the claims of his Gospel. It stands in sharp contrast to the kind of self-confessed obedience elicited by the commands of the centurion in the New Testament: 'I say to this one, "Go" and he goes, and to another "Come" and he comes, and to my slave, "Do this" and he does it.' (Matthew 8:8) So it takes a centurion from an imperialistic authority-structure to perceive this yet more excellent quality of authority in the person of Jesus. For obedience and authority belong together in the New

Testament. A Church will speak with true authority to the exact extent of its own willing and free obedience — and to the same extent as it sees itself also under authority.

Authority and the Gospel

'It may be,' the report continues, and again with something of the understatement, 'that authority of this kind is much harder to understand and obey than authority of a more imperious character. This is true and we glory in the appeal which it makes to faith.'[20] There is something glorious and characteristically Anglican (and it has to be said too, Gospel) about that kind of appeal, as there was also in a sense in Archbishop Runcie's lecture on the same subject at Trinity Institute, New York, in 1988. 'Paradoxically,' he said in a throwaway line, 'love is more powerful than power.'[21] It is of course the kind of remark which is largely lost to the legal mind, or in the kind of streamlined obedience of a Church part of which still persists in speaking of 'days of obligation' and 'fulfilling the obligation of the Sunday Mass'. It is the chemistry of Anglicanism in just this area of authority which is so distinctive — but also potentially so destructive. For the Lambeth 1948 report on authority urges upon our Communion the patience required by the scientific method of developing our understanding of truth. It urges a note of true pragmatism.

> 'Just as the discipline of the scientific method proceeds from the collection of data to the ordering of these data into formulae, the publishing of results obtained, and their verification by experience, so catholic Christianity presents us with an organic process of life and thought in which religious experience has been, and is, described, intellectually ordered, mediated, and verified.'[22]

So Anglicans point to this kind of thought for the continuous development of doctrine and practice, faith and order in their Churches.

'The experience is *described* in Scripture', the report tells us. 'It is *defined* in Creeds and in continuous theological study.' 'It is *mediated* in the Ministry of the Word and Sacrament.' 'It is *verified* in the witness of saints and in the *consensus fidelium.*'[23] Once again it must be said that such a process takes time and should necessarily resist steam-rollering and filibustering. And it must also be said that both liberals and traditionalists have been guilty in Anglican synods and conventions in recent years of precisely those accusations. The report rightly concludes:

> 'The Christ-like life carries its own authority, and the authority of doctrinal formulations, by General Councils or otherwise, rests at least in part on their acceptance by the whole body of the faithful, though the weight of this *consensus* does not depend on mere numbers or on the extension of a belief at any one time, but on continuance through the ages, and the extent to which the *consensus* is genuinely free.'[24]

As an ideal, it is ideal; but it has to be admitted that Anglican practice in this area in recent years has fallen far short of the ideal as laid out in that 1948 Lambeth report. In our discussions on the question of women's ordination, for example, have we pursued in our Churches the spirit let alone the letter of that clause? However, 'Eventually, the Church will reach a common mind,' cautions Archbishop Runcie, yet

> 'not easily or without controversy but steadily and surely so that what was opinion is tested and scrutinized and either rejected or eventually accepted as part of the continuing tradition of the Church in continuity with the past and in conformity with scripture.'[25]

Living with diversity

This inevitably means that in a fellowship of Churches such as we find in Anglicanism, we will not all be in step. Our varying cultures and constitutions will not encourage an impressive high-kicking goose step into the future (though it might also be said that the same drawbacks could save us from that headlong rush of the Gadarene swine which was also doubtlessly impressive to observers at the time). For there will necessarily be in Anglicanism a pluralism, yet as the Inter-Anglican Theological and Doctrinal Commission argues, such a 'pluralism can serve the cause of a deeper and fuller understanding of the Gospel, and so of a deeper and fuller unity in Christ.'[26] Anglicanism at its best rejoices in comprehensiveness for the sake of truth. That is to be sharply distinguished from its caricature — a compromise for the sake of peace.

Yet still the question has to be put: how can Anglicanism maintain the unity of the Spirit, faced as it is with increasing pluralism not only in its order and practice but in its doctrine and faith? 'No one will question' said Archbishop Runcie,

'that it has been the contentious issue of the ordination of women to the priesthood (and now episcopate) which has demonstrated an inadequacy in the central structures of the Anglican Communion. . . . This is not so much because the ordination of women (or the non-ordination of women) is itself a fundamental question at the heart of faith? — it is clearly not as central to the faith as, say, the doctrines of the Incarnation or the Holy Trinity. But different actions on this matter (as opposed to varied opinions) do threaten communion because the ordained ministry, and especially the episcopate, is the instrument of Communion.'[27]

If that is so, it is surely high time that some attention was given to strengthening those structures of worldwide Anglicanism, for the sake of maintaining unity and communion. A recent Anglican commission chaired by the Archbishop of Armagh has urged such a strengthening of structures through four main instruments in our worldwide and diverse Communion. These are, firstly, the Archbishop of Canterbury, who is still regarded as the 'personal symbol of unity' in the Communion. There is no attempt to elevate him or his chair to masquerade as an 'anglican pope' who addresses the Anglican Communion *ex cathedra*. It was Archbishop Davidson, not noted for his self-effacement, who nevertheless said that, 'Anything in the nature of a Canterbury Patriarchate would never receive the support' of the worldwide bishops. And it was Archbishop Coggan who reminded the bishops at Lambeth in 1978 that, although a kind of 'papal or patriarchal' head for Anglicanism had been discussed many times, he did not believe that such a concept belonged to the 'genius of Anglicanism'.[29] However, by history and tradition, the See of Canterbury focused in itself the symbol of both authority and unity.

The second instrument which has emerged and evolved is the Lambeth Conference itself, as a 'valuable forum where "the mind of the Churches" is discerned and expressed.' It is true that there have been many critics of the Lambeth Conference and many of them have advocated an international and more representative body along synodical lines in which the debates about faith and order in our Communion could be given a proper platform. But there is too some value in an episcopal Church calling together its episcopal leaders. Such a meeting will have an importance neither more nor less in extent than by what is represented at such meetings. It need not necessarily imply an hierarchical view either of authority or the episcopate. The Lambeth Conference is exactly what it is: an occasional meeting of the bishops from all the Provinces of the Anglican Communion.

The Archbishop of Armagh's paper advocated strengthening two further instruments in this quartet which would hopefully strengthen the themes of unity within diversity and pluralism within communion. The Anglican Consultative Council which is representative of the clergy and laity as well as the episcopate, while retaining its consultative nature should yet 'reflect more closely the pattern of representation of synodical bodies at local and provincial levels.'

'The Anglican Consultative Council exists' writes Bishop John Howe (and he should know, having headed it) 'to meet the increased pressures for the Anglican Communion to develop its role as one universal body within the Church.' Yet he goes on with some words of caution (and again perhaps Bishop Howe should know as well as anyone). 'Looking back over the Council' he says,

'and its antecedents one has the impression that the element of prophecy – even of "dream" as he called it – which derived from Stephen Bayne was present in the Anglican Consultative Council in its earlier years. More recently the element of vision has given place to a more overt concentration on efficiency as providing the way forward. How far this alteration is to advantage for the Council's undertakings is difficult to say. One is reminded at times of the phrase of Sydney Smith's in a different context, when he spoke of an "ungovernable passion for business". While the phrase may be taken as no more than a comment – Smith liked the man – it is also indicative of the danger to any ecclesiastical institution of declining in spirituality as it increases in either bureaucracy or nationalism.'[29]

Somewhat abrasive words, yet nevertheless a legitimate caution. Archbishop Michael Ramsey is reported to have been more to the point: 'It's into things it should not be!'[30]

Undoubtedly the Anglican Consultative Council will grow in the coming years, and necessarily so. Its London offices are now located in the same building as the missionary resources of the Church of England. That surely has to be a plus if something of missionary and evangelistic zeal can rub off upon the counsels of the Anglican Consultative Council!

However, in fairness, there has been an enormous increase in the amount of business handled by the ACC in recent years and efficiency and swift communication are integral in promoting life, witness and unity on a worldwide scale. Moreover, the recent meeting of the ACC in Singapore in 1987 lacked nothing in either vision or efficiency and had a spirit of mission, evangelism and ecumenism all clearly pointing to the kingdom and not simply to the institution of the Church. Such gatherings will be increasingly important and not less important in maintaining the unity of the Anglican community in the years ahead.

The fourth instrument in the structure of the Anglican Communion is the Primates' Meeting 'which provides opportunities for collegiality between those having special responsibility in individual provinces.'

Such then is the quartet or quadrilateral (another one) of instruments whose role it is to aid and to care for the unity of a widely diverse Communion in the face of tensions, conflict, change and crisis.

Controversy and Communion

'Differences are not sinful. They can be creative.' Archbishop Coggan reminded the bishops in his opening sermon in Lambeth 1978. 'The one thing that matters above all else, is that *nothing* shall break our love for one another.'[31]

Hence the emphasis among Anglicans on a 'Communion' which is so much more than a structure, an organization or even a fellowship. 'I believe it is important,' said Archbishop Runcie,

'that we Anglicans describe ourselves as a Communion. We rejoice in this, but we must not imagine that we need do nothing to maintain communion. Relationships need time, care and above all love if they are to flourish and develop. When strains arrive as in marriage — the institution of marriage itself gives space and freedom for healing, for self-restraint, for restoring communion between husband and wife.'[32]

Unity for a Christian is neither mathematical nor organizational: it is visionary, and is most clearly revealed to us in the very nature of the Godhead, whose unity and diversity is maintained by the communion of the Holy Spirit. Mankind — all mankind — bears something of the image of that unity, however scarred and distorted. The power structures of nations and between nations know little of this revealed mystery of unity, authority, power and obedience. And so our world is littered with hideous distortions in which individuals are suppressed for the sake of society or elevated out of all context in the name of individualism. Totalitarianism and suppressive regimes exist to the left and right of us, and the history of the Church itself contains whole chapters when we have imitated such blasphemous shortcuts to authority and unity in the name of neatness, tidiness and efficiency. The bully, either at the head of a large corporation or state, has known no better way to exemplify strength than by brute force, while the Inquisition and courts of the Churches have often simply reproduced these distorted images in the name of the Kingdom of God and His righteousness.

At its best, the Anglican Communion is an evolving fellowship of Churches from diverse cultures at different stages in their development. It could be given to such a Communion of Churches, albeit small and by worldly standards weak, to show the power of God and the wisdom of God as best revealed in the foolishness of mankind and the weakness of nations. To be an Anglican is a vocation within a vocation rather like the vocation to be a monk or nun is set within the wider vocation of baptism.

There will be those who find such patient and time-consuming deliberations and listening a frustration and a disappointment.

Nevertheless, 'a man's reach must exceed its grasp or what's a heaven for?', writes Robert Browning, and the caution to such impatience is still eloquently apposite in the words of Samuel Taylor Coleridge:

> 'He who begins by loving Christianity better than truth will proceed by loving his own sect or Church better than Christianity and end by loving himself better than all.'

The results of Lambeth 1988 may not impress the world at large. The press will not give banner headlines to a process of waiting upon God or to another step along the long road of Christian maturity. When Bishop Fulton Sheen was being pressed by journalists about division and conflict in Vatican II between conservatives and liberals, he is said to have replied along these lines (which would certainly not make headlines in the media):

> 'We must not speak of conservatives and liberals for these are political terms and quite inappropriate for the Church. In biblical terms there are two kinds of bishops — shepherds and fishermen. Shepherds care for the flock; fishermen launch out adventurously into the deep. We need both.'

Yes, we need both and not either/or. So in all our searchings we need to remember that truth is always beyond all our parties, our images and our concepts.

'So Anglicans,' writes David Edwards,

> 'cannot persuade anyone that they have worked out a system to which all should submit. On the contrary, through many controversies it has become clear that Anglicanism is a spirit, not a system — and that it is a spirit which involves a willingness to recognize that no neat formula can contain the biblical and Christian fullness . . . For here [in Anglicanism] is a small model which allows much diversity, theological and cultural in order to welcome truth and reality, even at the price of being, or of appearing to be, untidy, confused and broken; and here is an experiment (often a failure) which is admirable precisely because, when at its best, it has never claimed to have reached all the answers.'[33]

After all, systems express themselves through structures and structures frequently inhibit growth and freedom. On the other hand, spirit is expressed through a common union of one mind and heart. The model for the unity of the Church can be nothing less than the model of the communion of the Holy Spirit, who never seeks to glorify himself but always insists on pointing to Another, and to the further glory which has yet to be revealed.

REFERENCES

[1] *Anglican Information,* March 199, p. 1
[2] Stephen W. Sykes, *The Integrity of Anglicanism,* Mowbrays, London & Oxford, 1978, p. 88
[3] Crockford's *Clerical Directory,* 1987, Preface, p. 59
[4] Charles Moore, A.N. Wilson, Gavin Stamp, *The Church in Crisis,* Hodder & Stoughton, 1986, p. 132
[5] Ibid.
[6] Bernard Levin, *Synod and the Sinners,* London Times, Nov. 12th 1987
[7] Archbishop Runcie, *Many Gifts, One Spirit,* Church House Publishing, 1987, p. 14
[8] Lesslie Newbigin, *Foolishness to the Greeks,* William B. Eerdmans Publishing Co., 1986, p. 4
[9] Alec Vidler, *The Theology of F.D. Maurice,* London, 1945, p. 215
[10] William Oddie, 'Anglicanism at the Eleventh Hour', cited in *The Christian Challenge,* Volume XXVII, No. 1, p. 20
[11] Archbishop Runcie, Lecture II: 'The Anglican Response', Trinity Institute, New York, 1988
[12] Ibid., Lecture I, 'Authority in Crisis'
[13] Ibid.
[14] Ibid.
[15] *The Lambeth Conference 1948,* (London 1948), Par II, p. 84 ff
[16] Ibid.
[17] Ibid.
[18] Luke T. Johnson, *Decision Making in the Church — a Biblical Model*
[19] *The Lambeth Conference 1948,* (London 1948), Part II., p. 84 ff

[20] Ibid.
[21] Archbishop Runcie, Lecture II: 'The Anglican Response', Trinity Institute, New York, 1988
[22] The Lambeth Conference 1948, (London 1948), Part II, p. 84 ff
[23] Ibid.
[24] Ibid.
[25] Archbishop Runcie, Lecture II: 'The Anglican Response', Trinity Institute, New York, 1988
[26] Cited by Canon Van Culin at the Review Address for ACC-7, *Many Gifts, One Spirit,* Church House Publishing, 1987, p. 22
[27] Archbishop Runcie, Lecture II: 'The Anglican Response', Trinity Institute, New York, 1988
[28] James B. Simpson and Edward M. Story, *Discerning God's Will,* Thomas Nelson, 1979, p. 263
[29] John Howe, *Highways and Hedges, Anglicanism and the Universal Church,* Anglican Book Centre, Toronto, Ontario, 1985, p. 91
[30] James B. Simpson and Edward M. Story, *Discerning God's Will,* Thomas Nelson, 1979, p. 209
[31] Ibid., p. 262
[32] Archbishop Runcie, Lecture: 'The Anglican Response', Trinity Institute, New York, 1988
[34] David L. Edwards, *The Futures of Christianity,* Hodder & Stoughton Ltd, London, 1987, p. 111

CHAPTER FOUR

Limbering up for Lambeth '88

'It is such a tremendous thing to belong to the Church of God, and to know that you are loved, that you are upheld, that you are prayed for, and you know, as we've experienced it [in South Africa] that there is a wall of fire surrounding you. The forces of evil might sometimes be apparently on the rampage. And you are willing to be affirmed by your brothers at Lambeth who will remind you from their different contexts that this is God's world and He is in charge.'[1] Bishop Desmond Tutu

Great expectations!

'The warm-ups have started,' reported the *Church Times* at the beginning of 1988, 'the press corps is preparing its "Who's Who", Kent University is installing portocabins and telephones, clerical outfitters are getting ready for a roaring trade. . . .'[2] And what for? In readiness, of course, for Lambeth '88.

'I hope that the Lambeth Conference will not be seen as just another isolated conference which produces a report.' Bold and optimistic words by Archbishop Runcie back in 1983. 'This is why we have to begin now with our preparations', he continued. 'I hope that each bishop will be in close communication with his diocese about it and come reflecting its concerns.'[3] These words have continued to linger in the atmosphere over the five years leading up to Lambeth '88, 'I hope . . . that each bishop will bring his diocese with him.'

From the outset there was real commitment to preparing for Lambeth '88. If it proved to be the last such Conference (and there are all kinds of pressures and persons around who might for various reasons wish it to be so) there can be no doubt that the twelfth

Lambeth Conference gets the prize for preparation. More time, energy, research, pens, ink and paper, committee meetings and reports have gone into preparing for it than for any of its predecessors.

Back in 1987, Archbishop Runcie, addressing one of the several planning conferences for Lambeth '88, said to the assembled delegates from the twenty-eight Provinces of the Communion some stirring and encouraging words which proved to be even more true as July 16th, 1988, drew nearer.

> 'The expectations are running high for next year's Lambeth Conference. There is undoubtedly unprecedented interest and unprecedented attendance, and the thoroughness of the planning arrangements reflects a strong commitment to make it a memorable event in the life of our Communion.'[4]

And so it proved to be, for a mixture of reasons, but in no small way because of the high priority which Archbishop Runcie had given to Lambeth '88 and its preparation since the day he was enthroned in 1980.

The Archbishop of Canterbury

What printing was to the first Reformation, jet air travel, combined with television and the computer are to the 'reformation' that is going on in all the Christian Churches at the close of the twentieth century — it is the same 'Word' business! The most enterprising communications exercise undertaken by the reformers of the sixteenth century was to nail Luther's ninety-five theses to the church door at Wittenburg. Communication is surely the mortar for building community and it becomes more, not less, important across a wide diversity of climates, cultures and languages. Archbishop Longley, the chairman of the first Lambeth Conference in 1867, never left the continent of Europe in his long and somewhat sedentary life. Bishop Winnington Ingram was the first Bishop of London ever to visit America. It was Archbishop Fisher who was the first really 'jet-age' Archbishop of Canterbury, who went to see for himself something of the shape of the world outside the European Continent. He did this very much as an ambassador for Anglicanism. He and Mrs Fisher crossed the Atlantic in 1946 precisely in order to put 'the Lambeth Conference (1948) on the map',[5] as he expressed it. On that occasion they travelled by sea (not air) on the Mauretania, first visiting Canada where Fisher addressed all the bishops of the whole Synod of the Church of Canada in St John's Church at Winnipeg.

From Canada, Fisher went to the United States. He was to visit America no less than four times in the seventeen years of his primacy. He gave the keynote speech at the General Convention of the Episcopal Church in Philadelphia in 1946. He took the opportunity to spell out to the Church in the United States the implications of membership within, and commitment, to the Anglican Communion. 'The Anglican Communion,' he told his American audience,

> 'embraces many national Churches, provincial in name or character, and a large number of dioceses not yet organized as separate Provinces or national Churches. They are spread all over the world. The name Anglican is already a misnomer; it indicates their remote origin, but it does not at all describe their present condition. They are indigenous Churches, not only here and in England and in the British dominions, but in India, China, Japan, Ceylon, and Africa, East and West. Wherever they are, they stand for a particular tradition within the Holy Catholic Church of Christ and until that tradition is taken up into a wider fellowship, they must cohere.'[6]

Nothing less than the words of a crusader, albeit one from a very specific and in many ways very limited stable of a very, very English public school! Fisher subsequently visited other parts of the Anglican Communion, as an ambassador, on his visits to Australia, New Zealand and various parts of Africa. He visited Uganda in 1955 and in the same year consecrated four African bishops (all black) in Namirembe Cathedral. So it was that he began to develop that aspect of the work of an Archbishop of Canterbury which has subsequently grown and developed as each decade has gone by in the life of the Anglican Communion. Archbishop Ramsey took up this aspect of the Primate's work and so did Archbishop Coggan. Yet all three put together would not equal the extensive travel which Archbishop Runcie has undertaken in the years leading up to Lambeth 1988.

This development demands attention, appraisal and radical adjustment in the 'job description' of future Archbishops of Canterbury.

'We are confident,' stated Section Three of the 1978 Lambeth Conference,

'that by the turn of the century, the role of the Archbishop of Canterbury as the acknowledged focus of unity of the autonomous Churches of the Anglican Communion will make the international aspect of the appointment even more demanding both in time and leadership than it is at present. We recognize that this cannot but have implications for the Church of England and for the province and diocese of Canterbury.'[7]

It does and will increasingly do so. 'England has difficulty,' comments Bishop John Howe,

'in understanding the Archbishop of Canterbury's relation to the Anglican Communion. There is a tendency to regard him as a constitutional head with authority in all the Anglican Provinces rather than as the focus figure within a free family where authority rests with each Province and with its own Archbishop and Synod.'[8]

Nevertheless, the point still stands.

'When the Archbishop of Canterbury speaks and acts as the centre of affection and as the pastoral office in whom all the Churches of the Communion meet each other, he exercises his vocation both to gather the Church in council and to guide and assist the Church in witness, service, and in the preservation of its unity.'[9]

Undoubtedly, and on a greater scale than for any of his predecessors, this has been true for Archbishop Runcie and not least in preparing the whole Communion for Lambeth '88. Furthermore, as we have seen, in the papers prepared by the Archbishop of Armagh and his working party on the structures of Anglicanism (see page 81), the role and function of the successor to St Augustine of Canterbury takes its place as one of the four points in the structures of Anglicanism for the maintaining of unity within the Communion. Archbishop Runcie's monumental travels all over the world have undoubtedly 'paid-off' in preparing for the Lambeth Conference, but they have also been costly of his time and energy in a decade when there has been considerable turbulence back home for him in the English General Synod, in the media and in the rash of ecclesiastical squabbles which seem to have afflicted the Church of England unduly in the '80s.

The Anglican Consultative Council

Happily, an ever-stronger Anglican Consultative Council with its Secretary-General, Canon Sam Van Culin since 1983, certainly limbered up for Lambeth '88. Canon Sam Van Culin has been wearing several hats in preparation for the Conference. Not only does he head up his team of eleven colleagues in the ACC, he is secretary to the meeting of Primates (who have met more frequently of late) and also secretary throughout the days of talking (and one suspects throughout the nights of drafting) during the actual Conference. For all this he is an amazingly delightful and accessible person. Perhaps this graciousness is derived in no small way from his deep conviction that the Lambeth Conference must be one of the servants of the Anglican Communion and not its dictator.

By implication, therefore, the primary role and function discharged by him and his staff at the ACC is one of servicing this widely and increasingly diverse Communion. For Canon Van Culin it is clear that the Lambeth Conference 'crystalizes, animates and feeds the Church in a unique way.'[10] In preparation for Lambeth '88, Canon Van Culin has also clocked up a large amount of 'frequent-flyer' miles. He has made himself available on the speaking circuit, taking part in pre-Lambeth meetings for bishops with pre-Lambeth briefings in parishes, deaneries and dioceses around the world. Reflecting on these meetings, he concluded:

> 'If you listen carefully, whether it is in Tokyo, Nairobi, Singapore or Liverpool, the context may be different but the issues are the same wherever I travel. And they are — how to help people live a faith that is freeing and fulfilling and how to find your own vocation? How to sustain a fulltime paid ministry and how to develop the nonstipendiary ministry of the laity? These are all issues of considerable importance.'[11]

Meetings in general have been of the order of the day in the years leading up to Lambeth '88. The Anglican Consultative Council has met seven times in all, in various parts of the world. It is a widely representative body of lay men and women as well as bishops and archbishops, drawn from all five continents. In Singapore, at the seventh meeting of the ACC, there were also several observers from other Churches, together with some seventy-five participants served by a staff of fourteen and a communications' team of some half dozen.

Although the agendas for these meetings over the years have been wide-ranging, the Singapore meeting in 1987 was necessarily heavily loaded in the direction of preparing for Lambeth '88.

Archbishop Runcie preached at the opening service: 'How do we proclaim the gospel of reconciliation,' he asked the congregation,

'to all nations in the world divided into North and South, East and West, by poverty or politics, while the Christian Churches remain themselves divided and we Anglicans squabble over the ordination of women?'[12]

A somewhat rhetorical question, presumably deliberate in its overstatement (or even its oversimplification). Nevertheless it makes a valid and important point which the Lambeth Fathers would do well to heed. After all, his visits have exposed him to the scars and wounds of the world so that perhaps the words represented something of a real *cri de coeur.* He touched again on this world-view backdrop to the Lambeth Conference:

'We live in a world where agonizing decisions have to be made if what is now scientifically possible is to serve truly human values. New techniques in embryology face men and women of all faiths, and none, with new and difficult ethical questions. How do we recognize the Risen Christ in the medical scientist or the infertile couple who long for God's gift of children? But alongside new scientific possibilities there are also new and terrible diseases. How do we uphold standards of biblical chastity and fidelity and also proclaim the Gospel of God's suffering love to the young person dying of AIDS? And there is the age-old problem of hunger and the new debate about development. How do we proclaim Christ as the living Bread to the child dying of malnutrition?'[13]

What sort of Church — what sort of Conference?

Yet at the conclusion of his address, Archbishop Runcie focused upon the kind of Church he wanted to see — a Church which was sensitive to and aware of the needs of the world, North, South, East and West — the complex and painful world in which it was set and in which Lambeth '88 was summoned to serve.

'Some of you will know the book or the film, *A Room With a View.* It is the story of a young English girl's awakening on her first visit to Italy. On her return to England, Lucy's neatly ordered life is thrown off-balance. The conventional relationship with her family and fiancé is threatened by the spontaneous promptings of her heart for George, the man she comes to love in spite of the divisions of class and social background . . . . There are two Anglican clergymen at the end of E.M. Forster's novel, and for me they are parables of two kinds of Church,'

admitted the Archbishop.

'There is the Chaplain in Florence, the Reverend Cuthbert Eager: a consumate snob and puritan who despises George because his family are in Florence "for trade". Then there is Mr Beebe, of whom Lucy says, "He seems to see good in every one. No one would take him for a clergyman." It is Mr Beebe who intuitively sees that Lucy must break out of the conventional patterns of life which surround and entomb her. In Italy this does not quite happen, but Mr Beebe knows it will happen one day. He has noticed how passionately Lucy plays the piano and says this of her: "Does it seem reasonable that she should play so wonderfully, and live so quietly? I suspect that one day she will be wonderful in both. The watertight compartments in her will break down, and music and life will mingle."'

'Let Mr Beebe' concluded the Archbishop, 'be our model for the Church. A Church which allows life and music to mingle. A Church which encourages renewal, awakening and resurrection.'[14]

Powerful words! Clearly Archbishop Runcie wanted Lambeth '88 to be such a Church — a Church which 'encourages renewal, awakening and resurrection'. Perhaps he feels as he has gone around the Anglican Communion in the years leading up to the Lambeth

Conference that the Anglican Church so 'neatly ordered' (say in Fisher's day) is 'thrown off balance' in the 80's. The love of Christ must be released upon our world 'in spite of the divisions of class and social background'. Clearly it is Mr Beebe's kind of Church that he wants Lambeth '88 to manifest, a Church that will release the twenty-eight member-Churches of the Anglican Communion, like Lucy, 'to find her wings' and begin to use them. Such a burst of new life does not make for a 'neatly ordered life' as Archbishop Runcie knows to his cost.

Canon Sam Van Culin on the following day gave an equally spirited address with something of a masterly overview: a kind of 'state of the Churches' address. 'Mission,' he reminded all the delegates, 'exists within culture.'[15] Surely the Anglican Communion must extend into very different cultures with all the opportunities and challenges that such a view of worldwide mission necessarily demands. It was significant that the meeting of the ACC in the year immediately before Lambeth should have been convened in Asia. Again, Canon Van Culin reminded the council that Christianity was not

'a recent colonial import into Asia. It appeared in the heartlands of Asia as early as the sixth century A.D. The Anuradhapura Cross — a Nestorian Cross set on a lotus — found carved in a pillar which once held up the roof of a shopkeeper in Anuradhapura, North Ceylon, testifies to the existence of a Christian community before the fifth century. The Bishop of Kurunagala [it so happened present at the meeting of ACC-7] wears one.'

'On the Sian-fu tablet in China', Canon Van Culin continued,

'we find an eighth century summary of Christian doctrine and a review of Chinese Church history. Carved above this inscription is again a cross set on the lotus (a typical Buddhist symbol) while issuing from under it are clouds — also associated in popular Taoism with the sages. Christ the true sage sits on the throne of Buddha.'[16]

Or as the Archbishop of Adelaide has said somewhat more succinctly,

'Can Christians find in other faiths not only that which is not contrary to the Christian Gospel in much that they believe, but may there even be things that illuminate the Gospel for us in a way that we hadn't expected?'[17]

Easy of course to say it eloquently and to see it symbolically; quite another matter to carry such a vision into the deliberations of the Lambeth Conference and to apply it to all the cultures represented in the gymnasium of Kent University in the summer of 1988. Even more difficult perhaps to retain that vision and to make it a reality in the sixty-four thousand congregations of the Anglican Communion worldwide.

Communication: Lambeth '88

It becomes at the human level a massive communications exercise. To this end the ACC put out a lively twenty-minute video (again another 'first' for Lambeth '88) seeking to convey in visual, as well as in didactic terms, something of the challenge of the Lambeth Conference. It is a well produced and refreshing documentary, put together by professionals from eleven Anglican Provinces. *Lambeth '88 – The Call* was ready by March 1986 and was in general circulation by September of that same year.

'The call has gone out,' the video begins, 'preparations have begun for the twelfth Lambeth Conference of Anglican bishops. . . .'

What will they be doing and what's all the fuss about? The reply is much to the point. 'They [the bishops] will gather to pray, support and challenge each other and together seek the mind of Christ for the Anglican Church today.'[18] We were reminded of previous Lambeth Conferences, yet promised that Lambeth '88 would be a conference with a difference – an important difference because, or so we were assured, 'you will be included in the process. It is important that you [Anglicans all over the world] share your experiences, hopes and concerns with your bishop. Help him to bring his diocese with him to Lambeth '88.'[19]

And then in more prosaic words, the Archbishop of Canterbury took up the summons. 'We stand,' he said, 'at a juncture in the history of humankind where the issues which confront us are of a scale and a magnitude that put in question the whole future of God's world.'[20] Even as early as October 1985, the Archbishop of Canterbury went on to assure us, there had 'already been wide consultation in order that we may discover how we may assist people in the places where they are, over how these questions impinge on them.'[21]

The ACC who produced the videotape in preparation for Lambeth should surely consider a sequel or a follow-up to Lambeth, for the corollary of bishops taking their dioceses to Lambeth will be for the same bishops to take something of Lambeth back to their dioceses.

For what was clear from the outset of the preparations for Lambeth '88 was that the bishops needed to prepare themselves and their dioceses if the agenda, the discussions and the subjects discussed were to involve all the bishops from every part of the world. Until very recent times (and largely because of language difficulties) Lambeth Conferences have been dominated by the English bishops, with the American bishops coming in as a close second. Big bucks and large representation can easily tempt a spirit of imperialism to take over. Hence the need to make sure that what was to be discussed at Lambeth represented heartfelt concerns and issues coming out of five continents from the South as well as the North and from the East as well as the West. The preoccupation of the North and the West with the status of women in the Church needs to be set within a wider context of other concerns and agendas, where, for example, Christianity is a minority sect within nationalistic and fundamentalist Islam, ecumenism may become a matter of life and death and survival. Mission and evangelism under such politically repressive regimes puts the reordering of ecclesiastical furniture into a new and different perspective.

Thus, in the course of a number of meetings and in a variety of media, Archbishop Runcie presented his ideas and the four main themes for Lambeth '88. He spoke first to the Primates (Kenya, 1983) who endorsed the overall agenda set by those themes. In their turn, the provinces drew up an extended agenda for each heading and in its turn, the Anglican Consultative Council, heeding the Archbishop's injunction to each bishop to 'bring his diocese with him', began to coordinate working groups, study material and books for use in all the Churches of the Anglican Communion so that the whole Church might prepare for Lambeth '88.

Doing the homework

The result of all this was an impressive assembly of study material published and publicly distributed in good time for the Conference. Here again the preparation was on a scale hitherto unrealized at any of the other earlier Lambeth Conferences. Much of the study material was coordinated by Bishop Michael Nazir-Ali. He left his work as Bishop of Rawalpindi in the Church of Pakistan when invited to become one of the theological consultants for Lambeth '88 and a coordinator of studies in preparation for the Conference. This has proved to be an impressive appointment. Bishop Nazir-Ali was educated at the Universities of Karachi, Oxford and Cambridge — a fine trio on any score. But then he is an impressive communicator of Christian faith and theology, not least in the setting of other world religions. He insists that 'Indian theological education is the most developed in the Third World.'[22] His researches in the field of the comparative philosophy of religion and his special knowledge and experience of other faiths have equipped him to make a notable contribution to one particular Lambeth study document, *Toward a Theology for Inter-Faith Dialogue*. Bishop Nazir-Ali has been based at the Oxford Centre for Mission Studies in the months leading up to the Conference and has travelled extensively around the Anglican Communion.

So it is that the four main themes for Lambeth '88 were well-serviced from the outset, acting like dragnets to pull into Lambeth the large and small fish of local and cultural concerns. All these needed to be sorted out and sized up ready for the bishops to bite on hopefully with some relish once the Conference opened.

The four themes for Lambeth '88 were: Mission and Ministry, Dogmatic and Pastoral Concerns, Ecumenical Relations and finally, Christianity and the Social Order. As overarching themes one could scarcely improve upon them for they promise to encompass all the other concerns arising from those dioceses which, in some way, were to be represented in the summer days of English unpredictable weather on the campus site of that rural English university. Certainly few worlds could be further apart than the world of gentle affluence in middle-class Kent, and the world of terrorism, poverty, disease and famine represented by over five hundred men of different coloured skins bringing with them deeply different concerns. If the Conference were to work at all, everything depended, after the Holy Spirit, upon homework, preparation, study and discussion.

THE FOUR THEMES

Theme One: Mission and Ministry

'That is how to make new Christians,' Archbishop Runcie explained, 'how to nourish them in the faith and how we are to be salt and leaven in the society where God puts us.'[23] Put like that, the issues seem straightforward enough. Bishop Festo Kivengere, Bishop of Kigezi in Uganda, who was chairman of this section before his serious illness, expanded this theme into no less than five questions, the first of which was: 'What is the nature of Christian proclamation in a world where all authorities are questioned?'[24] From that somewhat daunting initial question the range of topics glances over the use of gifts in all the baptized; the spirit of renewal which is sweeping through all the Churches; the need to rescue renewal-experience from mere personal pietism and set it loose upon the world through ministry and compassion.

Then, of course, there are the questions about changing patterns 'in the shapes of the ordained ministry' to equip that ministry 'for mission in the world' in differing cultures. Once again, as in previous Lambeth Conferences, there is a growing concern about the role and office of the bishop. 'What do you consider to be the *missionary* task and functions of a bishop?' What indeed, when over and above all the other tasks and functions the bishops are expected to perform, most of them can rarely get their heads over the top of the piles of paper and administration stacked upon their office desks. There can be no lasting renewal which is not schismatic or divisive in an episcopal Church without the renewal of the office of the bishop. Clearly the Lambeth Conference in '88 needed to give some attention to this important question.

Then there is the question of the emerging ministry of healing. As early as September 1987, Bishop Morris Maddocks, who was the advisor for the Ministry of Health and Healing to the Archbishops of Canterbury and York, sent out a letter of personal greeting to all the archbishops and bishops attending the Lambeth Conference in 1988. He pointed out that since the previous Conference in 1978 the ministry (of healing) had 'undergone a period of growth'. As the outward and visible sign of renewal in the Churches, the healing ministry has developed in recent years, witnessing powerfully to the continuation of Christ's own ministry among his people. It is encouraging to see this aspect of ministry placed centrally at the heart of discussions on Mission and Ministry in Anglican gatherings today — not least at a Lambeth Conference.

Nevertheless, renewal, healing and mission have all been abused by Christians. 'Every good thing' said Bishop Kivengere,

> 'has many times been misused by those who really mean to promote it. We Christians have a genius to misuse good things — for instance the frames with which we work in mission. The traditions have a tendency to become so rigid that instead of becoming facilitators of mission they become deterrents of mission.'[25]

Yes indeed — 'What is rigid, gently bend; what is frozen warmly tend' is the ancient prayer to the Holy Spirit from the medieval mass — that same Holy Spirit who alone can release and empower true mission. For all mission comes directly from the heart of God Himself who is always sending out His people precisely because love always goes out of its way, and always has done. In 'these last days' God could do nothing less than *send* his only Son. 'The Lord Jesus could easily have remained comfortably in Nazareth, humanly speaking' continued Bishop Kivengere with that authentic power that is coming out of the Church in Uganda for the strengthening and encouraging of all the Churches. 'You know his years of ministry' Bishop Kivengere tells us from the heart, 'were on the move all the time. The Church, the community of the Risen Christ, a community of hope, cannot stand stagnantly without losing its identity. It's a community on the move to meet a needy world.'[26] (It is hard not to reflect that in all interviews with the bishops of Lambeth there is this big difference: bishops of the older Churches like England, America, Australia and New Zealand seem to begin their discussions from the base of the Church as an institution. The bishops from the developing countries and in particular from Africa and South America do not begin with ecclesiatical models for the Church and its problems. They always seem to start with the person of Jesus and move from him, his ministry, mission and Spirit to the life and witness of Christians today. Of course, like all generalizations one could fault this, but one should not perhaps ignore it. It seems to give to the newer Churches whether evangelical, charismatic or Anglo-Catholic in emphasis, a freshness and a directness which is most appealing.)

So Bishop David Sheppard, the Vice-Chairman of the Section on Mission and Ministry, tells us, 'We want to have a beautifully ordered worship and efficient Church life, but there are a great many people who are not able to hear it. Are there groups of people,' he asks us to consider, 'who are saying this Christ and this Church are not for me? If so, why are they saying it? Is our Church at home too much at ease in one culture and not at all in another?'[27]

No wonder that the discussions from all the many cultures represented at Lambeth ranged so widely under the apparently rather closed heading of Mission and Ministry.

Theme Two: Dogmatic and Pastoral Concerns

Dogmatic and pastoral concerns belong together. Belief begets behaviour: what we believe affects the way we try to live. 'The Church needs to have its faith right' insists the Archbishop of Adelaide, the Most Reverend Keith Rayner.

'It is not simply that credal orthodoxy is important for its own sake. The faith we hold determines our understanding of and relationship with God; shapes our worship; gives direction to our pastoral and evangelistic practice; affects our relationships with other Churches and other religions; and influences the way we live out our Christianity in daily life.'[28]

Yet in Anglicanism there is something of a crisis of faith. 'Many people assume' Archbishop Rayner said,

'that we have a faith that was once delivered to the saints and that goes on and doesn't change. And of course there is a real sense in which that's true. Yet the expression of that faith has to keep on changing because the world in which the Church is set is changing

99

all the time. New insights come as we study the scriptures more deeply and as light comes in from all kinds of secular knowledge.'[29]

Again, a new perspective comes to this discussion from the original Vice Chairman for this Section — Bishop James Yashiro, Bishop of Kita Kanto, Japan. In Japan he tells us,

'The number of Christians is less than one per cent, or maybe one-half of one per cent of the entire population. So the question is "how far can we be open to the people of other faiths without losing sight of the centrality of the Gospel of Jesus Christ?"'[30]

'It is clear that issues related to authority will be central', Archbishop Rayner warned us long before Lambeth '88 began.

'The classical Anglican tradition has been to accord the Bible a unique and central place but to acknowledge the role of tradition and reason in understanding it . . . It may be time for Lambeth to clarify and restate the Anglican understanding of these elements of authority.'[31]

No small undertaking, yet clearly central to Lambeth '88 and indeed to the survival and continuity of the Anglican Communion.

Theme Three: Ecumenical Relations

Archbishop Michael Peers, Primate of Canada, brought to Lambeth and the section of which he is chairman not only a remarkable facility as an outstanding linguist but also a passion for unity. 'For me personally,' he said,

'the issue is a very simple one . . . in the words of our Lord, that they all may be one . . . *"that the world may believe"*. The world in which I live believes less and less. I don't understand all of the reasons about that, but I am certain that the disunity of the Church is at least part of that and, if the world is to believe then I have to be about the business of the unity of the Church.'[32]

Again, this sounds very fine. But we need to ask what sacrifices need to be made for the sake of unity and whether the Church or its different provinces are ready to make them? Canada has been perhaps the most adamant part of the Anglican Communion in its insistence upon belief in the ordination of women to the priesthood and the episcopate. Has that step permanently put paid to any really serious further progress with the largest Church in Canada and indeed in the Western world? Bishop Buckle, the Assistant Bishop of Auckland in New Zealand, puts the question in precisely that way, though he may not have followed through *all* the implications of his own eloquence.

'The Church that lives to itself, dies by itself.' Well, we have heard that before, though it is no less true because it has been frequently stated. 'That's the unity question of Anglicanism today', Bishop Buckle tells us.

> 'Are we prepared to face toward the future for the Kingdom of God and be willing to offer those things which are rich within ourselves but equally to receive and in some way by God's grace, let go of those things that are perhaps less important?'[33]

Yet again the 'ten-thousand-dollar question' for the Anglican Communion needs to be put: for the sake of unity, to what must we hold fast and what can we afford to let go? All parts of our Church are littered with sacred cows — not only from tradition in the past but also from the contemporary and 'open-minded' cult of the present day.

This question was asked at the outset in its more theological and ecclesiological form by both the chairman and vice chairman for this section.

> 'The bishop is, in office and person, a sign of unity. The Church, indeed the world, has the right to expect that as a worldwide fellowship the bishops will also manifest that sign. What shall we offer "that they all may be one . . . that the world may believe?"'[34]

What indeed?

Theme Four: Christianity and the Social Order

Christianity and the social order is probably at the top of the issues for Lambeth '88. Lambeth Conferences through the years have not had an undistinguished record for tackling (often courageously) the larger questions concerned with the social order. It was the Lambeth Conference of 1930, between the two World Wars, which addressed questions as wide-ranging as birth control, racism, justice and peace. Yet is it possible to begin in any realistic way to deal adequately, in the few days permitted for discussion, with such important questions at Lambeth? Of course in many ways this is an ongoing agenda for most of the Churches most of the time. 'To bring the discussion of social issues within manageable proportions it will be focused in this section around the general theme of human rights and responsibilities,' said the Archbishop of York, John Habgood, and Archbishop Desmond Tutu in a joint statement. 'The two main areas of concern will be the nation state and the family, and the conflicts which arise in relation to these in a divided and rapidly changing world.'[35]

On another occasion, a video interview, Archbishop Habgood focused this section even more tightly.

'What we are going to try and do is to break this down into two major sections. The dominant theme of the whole thing will be "Majority and Minority: Rights and Responsibilities". And so we shall be trying to think of how majorities can treat minorities fairly — whether that majority is a large nation looking at a small nation, or a large group within a nation. And then we will also be trying to look at some of the issues affecting families and the sort of pressures on families in a rapidly-changing world.'[36]

It was under this last section that it became clear in preparing for Lambeth '88 (as it had been in previous Lambeth gatherings right back to 1867) that the question of polygamy had to be addressed. Back in 1986 a special committee was appointed by the conference of Anglican Provinces in Africa to study the controversial issue of polygamy and the Christian family in both its theological and pastoral dimensions. The issue has been over many years a subject for heated debate in over forty African Churches. *Anglican Information* commented in its issue of September 1986 that 'The pastoral debate on the Church's role in a predominantly polygamous culture has been evident since the coming of the missionaries to Africa.' It certainly has. It was deliberately and rather carefully pushed under the carpets in Lambeth Palace by Archbishop Longley at the first Lambeth Conference in 1867. 'The debate has intensified', warned *Anglican Information*, 'after the indigenization of Christianity and the slow and cautious acceptance of monogamy by many African societies . . . The faithful who participate in a polygamous marriage institution have found it extremely difficult to gain total acceptance from the Church. Such faithful are barred from full participation. For example, they do not receive the sacrament, ostensibly because they are, in the eyes of the Church, not properly "wedded". They even find themselves in a situation where their offspring cannot be baptized, again for the same reason. Neither can they receive a Christian burial.'[37]

Clearly a conspicuous and heroic figure in Lambeth '88 was the Vice-Chairman of this Section, Archbishop Tutu — a truly household name throughout the whole world in the 1980's. With simplicity and totally disarming honesty, Desmond Tutu spelled out something of what this whole section of Lambeth should necessarily tackle in its deliberations.

'The question of relationship is so important . . . If I am aware that I am not just "my brother's keeper" I am "my brother's brother", then the effect of spending obscene amounts of money on the arms race when people are starving, when a fraction of that amount would assure that our children would have a wholesome life and so on, I mean, is seen for the awful evil that it is.'[38]

Yet he went on to affirm that his passion for justice and peace was rooted firmly in and sprang directly out of his faith in a living God.

'It is precisely because I encounter — or I hope I encounter — God in the Eucharist, in meditation, that I am concerned about injustice and oppression and am afraid that God's children are being treated as even less than what they are.'[39]

So this section of the Conference was preparing for the discussion of issues ranging from world poverty to the problems of large urban communities; from bioethics to homosexuality. Indeed the Churches, especially in England and America, seem to have spent inordinate amounts of time and paper on the whole question of homosexuality in the months leading up to Lambeth. They not only considered its lifestyle as an alternative to the family, but also whether self-confessed 'practising' homosexuals (whatever that may mean) should be ordained — presumably both male and female homosexuals. Inevitably many of these discussions were vitiated by the outbreak of AIDS not only in America, the UK and Europe, but also in Africa where it is endemic and threatens to kill millions of Africans by the close of the century. Indeed for Bishop Holloway of Edinburgh, Scotland, it was an issue which was top of his agenda, coming as he does from a city where AIDS has a growing hold on the population.

Yet it was Desmond Tutu again who had perhaps the most telling observation as he prepared for Lambeth '88. 'It is such a tremendous thing to belong to the Church of God,' he told us,

'and to know that you are loved, that you are upheld, that you are prayed for, and you know, as we've experienced it [in South Africa] that there is a wall of fire surrounding you. The forces of evil might sometimes be apparently on the rampage. And you are willing to be affirmed by your brothers at Lambeth who will remind you from their different contexts that this is God's world and He is in charge.'

Surely that is a rather different and a rather wonderful expectation for a Lambeth Conference, and one we should never forget or weigh lightly. Archbishop Tutu went on to remind us (and perhaps it takes someone coming out of the violence and the evil which he witnesses to bring this point home to us more easy-going Christians in the northwest) that, 'Nothing,' he said, 'could have been more hopeless in the eyes of the world than Good Friday. And then Easter happened and WOW!' Then his eyes flashed with the fire of hope and joy as he put the question: 'Who could ever cease from being forever thereafter a prisoner of hope?'[40]

The power of prayer

The appointment of a chaplain for the 1988 Lambeth Conference was no formal, pious appendage to the whole exercise. It would seem from the outset to be the very heart of the matter: to call the whole Church to prayer, that quality of prayer which in spite of the problems and crises is eager to expect great things from God. 'All we can do is nothing worth', we often sing in a well-known Anglican hymn 'except God blesses the deed'. There was a happy accident of typographical error in the 1986 *Anglican Cycle of Prayer.* This little booklet sets out on a daily and weekly basis intercessions which cover the whole Anglican Communion – its Provinces, Churches, bishops and faithful. On the spine of that particular edition the misprint, instead of reading 'Anglican Cycle of Prayer', read 'Anglican Cycle of Power'.

'Now that's it in a nutshell', said Bishop Alistair Haggart, the appointed chaplain to Lambeth '88. 'We want the Anglican Cycle of Prayer for the Lambeth Conference to be an Anglican Cycle of Power!' 'The success of the Lambeth Conference depends on your prayers', the Churches throughout the world were reminded in the specially-produced videotape long before the Conference began. It was prayer then and involvement with the local bishop which were prized so highly as appropriate preparation for July 16th, 1988, 'so that the experience of Lambeth might begin' right where Anglicans find themselves in all five continents throughout the world.

Communication, conference and consultants

Yet in all of this, before, during and after the events at Kent University in July and August '88, communication remains the name of the game. To this end, the excellent publication *Anglican Information,* which is produced quarterly from the ACC office in London and edited by Robert Byers, has become an attractive, readable and rich resource for any who would wish to know more about the evolving life of the Anglican Communion. It is precisely what it claims to be, *information.* In the run up to Lambeth '88 it gave profiles of some of the newest of the twenty-eight Provinces, highlighting the kind of issues and concerns that a particular Province would wish to bring to Lambeth.

For example, perhaps it is important for Episcopalians from America as well as Anglicans from Europe and elsewhere, for whom the West Indies are something of a playground, to know that their Church is strong in those islands, yet that poverty is top of the agenda for the bishops who come to Lambeth from that Province. 'The

Anglican Church arrived in the West Indies with the original English settlers in the early part of the seventeenth century . . . The first two dioceses, the Diocese of Jamaica and the Diocese of Barbados, were created in 1824', *Anglican Information* tells us. The story evolves. Today there are eight dioceses. From a Church which was largely embassy-Christianity, the Church in the West Indies has, since 1959, become a self-governing province with nearly one million Anglicans and its own fully representative synod with three houses. The Church of the Province of the West Indies has had and continues to have a strong programme in education and schools. Yet it is the electronic church and the sectarian movement which are high up on the agenda of concerns from this Province.

The same *Anglican Information* goes on to tell us of the newest Province of the Anglican Communion — the Province of the Southern Cone, in South America. It is hard to believe that until as late as 1974 the Anglican dioceses in South America at the Southern Cone were all extra-provincial dioceses under Canterbury. In April 1983, at a special service at St John's Cathedral, Buenos Aires, the Anglican Church of the Southern Cone was inaugurated (Iglesia Anglicana del Cono Sud de America). What on earth is it like to be an Anglican, one might well ask, in Latin America? Bishop Adrián D. Cáceres tries to tell us: 'It is true,' he says with disarming honesty,

> 'that this Church has kept itself on the edge of the Latin American reality; that its ministry has not reached out further than its altars; that its attitude had been a stumbling block to those who want to be a neighbour to the wounded man, robbed and left on the roadside. In spite of this, the commitment remains with its duty impelling it to the fulfilment of the Gospel of love that it preaches and witnesses.'[41]

An especially significant pre-Lambeth Conference was held in November 1987 — The Latin-American Anglican Congress, which was convened in Santa Clara, Panama. It was the first time that members of the twenty-seven dioceses of the Spanish- and Portuguese-speaking nations had met and conferred. These dioceses reflected the total spectrum of Anglicanism and if party labels were appropriate (which they should not be) we would speak of evangelical, anglo-catholic and liberal colourings reflected at this congress. Bishop Colin Bazley spoke warmly of the experience of this gathering.

A tale of two cities:
the problems facing Anglicanism in South America
a slum on the outskirts of Sao Paulo, Brazil

'Our goal was met. We were successful in being able to communicate our differences and there was a pronounced spirit of joy in all our diversity. In language, churchmanship and cultural colouring the diversity represented at that conference was something of a miniature of the kind of diversity which was to be experienced in the Lambeth Conference of 1988.'

Then there is news of the important role the Anglican Bishop of Hong Kong is taking as Hong Kong prepares to come under the sovereignty of China in 1997, when the British government's lease of Hong Kong expires. The Anglican Diocese of Hong Kong has twenty thousand members with thirty-three parishes and missions together with a large number of schools. Bishop Peter Kwong is playing a major role in the deliberations leading up to 1997 and is also preparing the diocese to be a truly evolving Church looking to China for its cultural colouring, while remaining in the Anglican Communion.

These are all only small cameos and glimpses of the diverse concerns represented by the bishops at Lambeth in 1988. The face of the Anglican Communion is changing all the time. Yet a family or a fellowship always needs to strengthen its network of communication as it grows and extends in diversity. This is a large and important task. It is what is going on *between* the Lambeth Conferences in the way of communication which insures the success and fruitfulness of any particular three weeks or so set aside for each decennial Conference.

So in the years leading up to Lambeth '88 there has been a succession of mini-conferences for various groups within the Communion. These have ranged from the meetings of the Primates (which will remain a continuous feature of pan-Anglican life) to meetings of Provincial Secretaries held in London in October 1987, to a meeting of the senior communicators from around the Anglican Communion who came together to talk with each other about communication and to prepare to lend all their skills to doing a good job in communicating the events of Lambeth 1988 to the wider Church, other Churches and the world at large.

In January 1988 there was another first for Lambeth '88 – the first international conference for 'Young Anglicans'. This was held at Stranmillis College, Belfast, in Northern Ireland, a part of the world that none could visit without being aware of the ever-present reality of terrorism, violence and disunity in our Churches and in our world. In that setting the young delegates (some two hundred and fifty in all) discussed the four Lambeth themes. The Archbishop of Canterbury addressed them in St Ann's Cathedral, Belfast, on the Feast of the Epiphany. 'In many parts of the world,' he told them, 'I see a new movement of the Spirit giving fresh energy and enthusiasm in worship and fellowship. . . . This renewal of the Church has given great encouragement to many Christians and many congregations have found new life and inspiration. But sometimes,' he warned them, 'new-found faith can . . . fail to take seriously the world around us. Renewal in spirit must lead us on to renewal of mind . . . I have great expectations' he concluded 'that you have something special to give to the Church leaders who will come not only as Anglicans but from every denomination to Canterbury' for Lambeth '88[42].

Perhaps one of the most important pre-Conference conferences was the African pre-Lambeth conference held in the Limuru Conference Centre, Kenya, in July 1987, just one year before Lambeth '88. It brought together seven primates and fifty-one bishops from the African continent. 'The hope of the consultation was to formulate an African perspective so that the bishops could speak with a common voice and mind at the Lambeth Conference in 1988.'[43] In the environment of that smaller conference, it was possible for the African bishops to articulate the 'many problems facing Africa' and to highlight three basic issues: 'Food Production, the Population Explosion and Refugees'. Clearly AIDS was also an important topic for consideration by the African bishops. 'A most informative paper on AIDS was presented by Dr William Kornange, Permanent Secretary, Minister of Science and Technology.' The paper 'attempted to inform, rather than frighten, and cautioned religious leaders to begin an earnest and honest programme of social responsibility in the Church and family.' It was at this meeting that the special commission formally appointed to prepare a paper on polygamy also presented its report.

It is not difficult in all this welter of discussion, papers, conferences and communications in the lead up to Lambeth, to appreciate the need for specialist consultation. No one in their right mind would wish to pretend that a meeting of bishops whether in Africa, South America or at Kent University, will have at its fingertips all the specialist knowledge — theological and otherwise — that is clearly needed as such wide-ranging themes are explored. There is no suggestion in any ordinal (thank goodness) that the rite of consecrating a bishop confers upon the role or the office the nature of a polymath. Polymaths went out with the Middle Ages as indeed, hopefully, did prelacy.

Many of the bishops attending Lambeth are at the end of their ministries — indeed some of them are also at the end of their wits in the light of the agendas and concerns which surround them. More than a handful of the English bishops will immediately announce their retirement after Lambeth '88. Some, doubtless, will do so with a sigh of relief — at least they will not be around in office in the Church which is evolving through and after Lambeth '88! It will become somebody else's headache! Some bishops from elsewhere will quite honestly view the prospect with apprehension or a sense of routine indifference as they come to Lambeth hoping that there will be some time before, during or after the Conference for visiting London or for more social events together with their wives. Yet for those bishops who want to study, read and prepare for the Conference, Lambeth '88 offered the widest selection of well-produced reading material, coming out of working parties and study groups which were well serviced with specialist consultants. If authority is at root the basic question for Lambeth '88 then all bishops present would have had the opportunity to study the excellent volume on *Authority in the Anglican Communion* edited by Stephen Sykes. *The Emmaus Report* produced in digestible form the latest situation on the ecumencial front. All these publications went out in good time to all the Churches so that it was possible to have local translations of the material and to use the material in local diocesan meetings of preparation.

And so it has gone on for a solid two years before Lambeth — and always with the help and input of specialist consultants. Several women, including two women priests, were deliberately appointed as part of the panel of consultants in attendance at Lambeth.

In all, as 17th July 1988 drew nearer, nearly twelve hundred people from all over the world, in their varying capacities, began to converge upon the small city of Canterbury, in Kent. For the first time bishops from Churches in full communion with Canterbury — like the Churches of North and South India, the Church of Pakistan, the Old Catholic Church, the Church of Bangladesh and the Independent Philippine Church were members of the Lambeth Conference. Furthermore, a simultaneous translation service was available in English, French, Japanese, Spanish and Swahili.

Yet at the heart of the Conference, there was worship — and worship which reflected the varying liturgical rites throughout the Communion.

Of course there are bound to be those who will ask, 'Why this waste?' In other words — what does it cost? The Body of Christ needs love, care and attention today just as much as it did during the earthly incarnation of its Lord. 'Surprisingly, Lambeth Conferences come cheap. The Roman Catholic Church in just one country invests more in one papal visit than the whole Anglican Communion invests in a single Lambeth Conference every ten years'.[44] In other words, 'the bill', picked up by the whole Communion was in fact only a little over three quarters of a million pounds. Cheap at the price.

The end of the beginning

'Lambeth helps to draw us together', says Canon Sam Van Culin. 'It is a most effective animator. The ACC does a serious piece of work for the Communion, but it does not have the dramatic effect of a Lambeth Conference.'[45]

And all this in preparation for the moment — not unlike Canterbury pilgrims of Chaucer fame — when the great west doors of Canterbury Cathedral are opened wide to receive bishops from every continent of the world into its sacred environment of worship, prayer, witness and martyrdom. So they come. For even the most cynical it is a moment charged with emotion, colour, even pageantry, great with expectations that as the doors of the cathedral stand open to the wider environment outside that church building, so also the minds and hearts of those bishops attending Lambeth '88 will be opened wider still to the environment of the Kingdom of God which is always beyond the Church; extending it arms with new generosity, richer grace and deeper charity.

So they come — again like Chaucer's pilgrims — with their stories to tell, some doubtless expecting to make a mark, wanting to make a point, or even to score a point! Blindness and stupidity will doubtless have their part to play in as far as the gathering is human. Yet in as far as the gathering in Canterbury Cathedral on 17th July was part of the one holy, catholic and apostolic Church founded by Jesus Christ, it is to that extent the humble yet confident inheritor of the promise made to those first timid, stupid yet graced apostles — 'Lo, I am with you always, even to the close of the age.' Even so, come Lord Jesus.

[1] *Lambeth '88 — The Call,* (videotape), Anglican Consultative Council, London, 1988

[2] Nicola Cume, 'For The Church Times', *Anglican Information,* March 1988

[3] *Anglican Information, December 1983*

[4] Blackheath Conference, 1987

[5] William Purcell, *Fisher of Lambeth,* Hodder & Stoughton, 1969, p. 177

[6] Ibid., p. 179

[7] John Howe, *Highways and Hedges, Anglicanism and the Universal Church,* Anglican Book Centre, Toronto, Ontario, 1985, p. 105 ff

[8] Ibid., p. 106

[9] Canon Sam Van Culin, *Many Gifts, One Spirit,* for the ACC, 1987, Church House Publishing, p. 24 ff

[10] *Anglican Information,* March 1988, p. 1

[11] Ibid., p. 8

[12] *Many Gifts, One Spirit,* Church House Publishing, for the Anglican Consultative Council, 1987, p. 12 ff
[13] Ibid.
[14] Ibid.
[15] Ibid., p. 18 ff
[16] Ibid.
[17] *Lambeth '88 — The Call,* (video), Anglican Consultative Council, London, 1988
[18] Ibid.
[19] Ibid.
[20] Ibid.
[21] Ibid.
[22] *Anglican Information,* September 1987, p. 7
[23] *Lambeth '88 — The Call,* (video), Anglican Consultative Council, London, 1988
[24] *Anglican Information,* March 1987, p. 4
[25] *Lambeth '88 — The Call,* (video), Anglican Consultative Council, London, 1988
[26] Ibid.
[27] Ibid.
[28] *Anglican Information,* March 1987, p. 4
[29] *Lambeth '88 — The Call,* (video), Anglican Consultative Council, London, 1988
[30] Ibid.
[31] Special article written for *The Anglican Digest* by Archbishop Rayner
[32] *Lambeth '88 — The Call,* (video), Anglican Consultative Council, London, 1988
[33] Ibid.
[34] Ibid.
[35] *Anglican Information,* March 1987, p. 5
[36] *Lambeth '88 — The Call,* (videotape), Anglican Consultative Council, London, 1988
[37] *Anglican Information,* September 1986, p. 6
[38] *Lambeth '88 — The Call,* (video), Anglican Consultative Council, London, 1988
[39] Ibid.
[40] Ibid.
[41] Bishop Adrián D. Cáceres, *Crossroads Are for Meeting,* S.P.C.K., USA, 1986, p. 284
[42] Archbishop Runcie, Address in Belfast Cathedral, January 6, 1988
[43] *Anglican Information,* November 1987, p. 1
[44] Ibid., March 1988, p. 8
[45] Ibid.

PART TWO

Where Horizons Meet — Lambeth '88

CHAPTER ONE

 Canterbury Tales: The Faces of Anglicanism at Lambeth '88

> *'We have come together so that this Communion may be known by us in a real and personal way as we meet face to face. We have come to share, to learn, to listen, and then to search for words that will guide and encourage our Churches. We have come expecting God to do great things, in us and through us and in spite of us.'*
>
> Archbishop Robert Runcie
> Address at Inaugural Eucharist, Lambeth '88

Converging on Canterbury

It was raining, of course!

But then it had rained in England every day since the beginning of July. It was no surprise, therefore, that Sunday 17th July, 1988, should begin with rain for the 525 bishops, together with their wives, assembled in Canterbury. Along with consultants, advisors, staff and media, numbering some twelve hundred in all, the bishops had been arriving over the past few days and had been formally welcomed the previous evening to the twelfth Lambeth Conference, which was to last for three weeks from 17th July until 7th August. 'I look forward to enjoying this Conference and I hope you do', Archbishop Runcie had told the assembled bishops on Saturday evening at the formal welcome held in the large gymnasium at Kent University just outside Canterbury. 'I welcome you because the Lord has called us together and He is faithful.' Speaking a short welcome in French, Spanish, Japanese and Swahili, the Archbishop made it clear from the start that the Conference was taking seriously the wide variety of race, culture and language represented by the bishops arriving from the twenty-eight Provinces of the Anglican Communion. A simultaneous translation service available in four languages during all plenary sessions was no mere technological affectation.

Briefing the press on Saturday evening at the outset of the Conference, and wishing, as he said, to 'speak from the heart and not give a dreary rehearsal', the Archbishop of Canterbury had commented, somewhat whimsically, on the text from the Book of Acts where Paul met with crowds in Ephesus: 'Now some cried one thing, some another; the assembly was in confusion and most of them did not know why the assembly had come together!'

Yet come together they had — all the way to Canterbury as pilgrims through the ages have done since before the days of Chaucer.

The week before the Lambeth Conference leading Anglican charismatics from around the world had 'come together'. They knew why they had come to Canterbury: to nerve themselves for what they believed to be *the* challenge to the Church at the close of the century: 'the task of world evangelization'. Ten years earlier, just before the '78 Lambeth Conference began, a similar gathering had assembled with much euphoria to share 'renewal' — that much overused word of the '80s. The '88 gathering, while not lacking in enthusiasm for renewal, pointed forward to the need for another word of challenge for the whole Church: evangelization. 'After a decade of renewal,' said Canon Michael Harper, 'the Lord is calling us to a decade of evangelization.' That conference certainly seemed to know why it had come together — to share with gratitude the vitality and growth of the Church in the 'two-thirds world'; to request that evangelists and teachers from the developing countries come to the West bringing with them the message of Christ, which, ironically, had first been exported from the shores of the UK, the USA and the affluent West.

Other early arrivers were the Primates from the twenty-eight Provinces who had gathered at Lambeth Palace for twenty-four hours of quiet and retreat in preparation for the three weeks talking at Lambeth '88. Archbishop Runcie confessed at the press briefing on Saturday evening that the occasion had been a happy time together which seemed to augur well for high morale on the part of all those who would be arriving at Canterbury to attend the Conference. As he stood flanked by Canon Samuel Van Culin, the Conference Secretary, and Bishop Ronald Bowlby of Southwark, the 'Episcopal Co-ordinator for Communications Lambeth 1988', the welcoming panelists cut a confident picture for the beginning of a Conference which had been hailed with a mixture of forebodings and misgivings.

The American bishops had just come hotfoot from the heat, oppression and depression of Detroit and their Triennial General Convention. Similarly, the English bishops arrived somewhat weary from yet another meeting of their General Synod: they have three a year which sometimes seem to create more problems than they solve. The Afro-Anglican bishops had also been meeting. They came straight from this meeting at Cambridge (14th—16th July) with what they called a 'Cambridge Declaration' all at-the-ready to release on the rest of their Lambeth colleagues.

Also arriving (in the rain of course) were forty women from Africa, Canada, the Caribbean, Central and South America, and the Philippines. They came to be known as the Episcopal Women's Caucus (EWC, which is not at all the same as ECW — American's please note). They took up residence in Canterbury to celebrate the ministry of women already ordained in the Anglican Communion (to date something over a thousand in all) and to offer a series of lectures, seminars, worship and hospitality throughout the first part of the Conference. Along with other women, they were to make an outstanding contribution to the Conference on an evening specially set aside in the second week for women's reflections upon the Lambeth themes.

Also to Canterbury came the wives of many of the bishops. In 1978 they had met for only one week. Lambeth '88 was to hold their attention at their own specially arranged conference for the whole three weeks. Later, about three dozen Anglican Peace Pilgrims converged on Canterbury. Enthusiastic members of the Episcopal Peace Fellowship (USA) and the Anglican Pacifist Fellowship (UK) left Southwark Cathedral for Canterbury five days before the Lambeth Conference was due to begin. 'It was a great experience', explained John Pottle, a young man from Ithaca, New York, as a peal of bells rang out from the cathedral to welcome the pilgrims. *They* knew why they had come to Canterbury. They had come to deliver to the Vice Dean of the cathedral a declaration urging the Lambeth Fathers to take several actions to 'direct the Church in the quest for peace'.

To add to all of this, the Archbishop of Canterbury appointed for the first time Youth Consultants to advise the Conference on youth concerns. Vanessa Mackenzie from Southern Africa and Andrew

Masterton from Australia had been chosen by Dr Runcie after the International Youth Conference in Belfast in January 1988. 'Youth', said Archbishop Eames of Armagh at that conference, 'is the Church of today, not of tomorrow.'

All these people and many more besides — pilgrims with hearts 'devout, ready for Canterbury to set out' (Chaucer) — gradually arrived at the university to take up their three weeks' residence. The city of Canterbury became a festive city, although perhaps the present incumbent of the See of Canterbury would not wish to go quite as far as his esteemed predecessor, Archbishop Frederick Temple (1821 −1902), who made the somewhat exaggerated claim that it was 'the bounden duty of every ... man and woman to visit Canterbury at least twice in their lives.' Back in Chaucer's day, 'the rooms and stables were well kept and wide'. Today the student accomodation at the University of Kent, while 'well-kept' might have been a little on the narrow side, perhaps, for some of the American bishops and their wives. To other Episcopal visitors and pilgrims from less affluent nations, like the four bishops from Burma who arrived with only $14 between them, the accomodation doubtless appeared cheerful, ample and even luxurious.

All Dressed Up and No Place to Go

Yet still it rained, although as the hour for the opening service in Canterbury Cathedral drew nearer, the rain degenerated into that drizzle so characteristic of the English climate.

In one way or another, no less than 2,100 people found their way into Canterbury Cathedral on Sunday morning for the opening service. Floodlit by night, and gracefully presiding over the life of the city by day, the Cathedral and Metropolitical Church of Christ, Canterbury, houses the seat of Augustine, built of purbeck marble and dating from about 1220. Successive Archbishops have been enthroned in it through the centuries. 'Why should the Anglican bishops come all this way to meet at Canterbury at a conference presided over (however sensitively) by the Archbishop of Canterbury?' Might not some of the participants have felt resentment at the location and style of Lambeth Conferences? Archbishop Davis, Primate of New Zealand, to name but one, wanted to question the location of the Conference.

117

He felt that the English Church lacked 'an awareness of the breadth of the Anglican Communion. The fact that the Lambeth Conference meets in England reinforces and underlines this.' Referring to the role of the Archbishop of Canterbury, Davis commented somewhat perversely: 'Is it necessary for him to chair all the meetings?' The truth is he didn't.

'Is it necessary however to come to Canterbury? Yet they came and have come in increasing numbers for twelve such Conferences over the last 120 years. The first procession to enter the cathedral formally, a good half-hour before the opening service was due to begin, was that of the 'consultants' as they were termed. The patient crowd, gathered in the rain to watch this event, seemed singularly unimpressed and unexcited by this strange little procession. But then the face of theological reflection has seldom impressed or excited crowds throughout history. It is not really an observer's sport. So who were these consultants? Well, there were some twenty-six of them — seven women of whom two were women priests: the Revd Nan Peete, a black priest from Los Angeles, and the Revd Margaret Wood from New Zealand. The consultants were in some ways the 'theological heavies' who had a largely hidden yet nonetheless helpful contribution to make to the Conference. They included Professor Stephen Sykes, Regius Professor of Divinity at Cambridge, who has written distinguished works on the major themes underlying this Conference and who is notably an authority on Anglicanism; Elizabeth Templeton, author of *The Nature of Belief* who was to make a powerful contribution in one of the major presentations to the Conference in the first week; Professor Rowan Williams, Lady Margaret Professor of Theology at Oxford; plus theologians from South Africa, Costa Rica, Australia and Canada, together with Professor Henry Chadwick, presently Master of Peterhouse, Cambridge.

Then followed the observers and representatives of the other Churches. Orthodox clergy (whether bishops or priests) even in what Italian Roman Catholic prelates delight to call '*habito piano*' are rather more impressive to look at than theologians! The interest of the crowd clearly increased by several decibels as some of the top brass of the various Orthodox Churches came into sight. Officially there were some thirty observers from the Orthodox, Protestant and Roman Catholic Churches, as well as representatives from the World Council of Churches, the World Alliance of Reformed Churches, the

Lutheran World Federation and the World Methodist Council. Together with Dr David Russell from the Baptist World Alliance and representatives from the General Conference of Seventh Day Adventists and the Disciples of Christ Ecumenical Consultative Council, the ecumenical spectrum coming to Canterbury was broadly based, very colourful and warmly welcomed by Archbishop Runcie. At the first Lambeth Conference of 1867 it had been strictly Anglicans only. Happily, relations between all the Christian Churches have developed and deepened since those days, so that today a Lambeth Conference without representatives from other Churches would be unthinkable.

Next in the procession were those bishops in full communion with Anglican Churches, again a colourful bunch, clearly attracting the attention of the crowd. Bishops from the Churches of South India and North India, Pakistan and Bangladesh; the Old Catholic Churches, the Philippine Independent Church and the Mar Thoma Syrian Church of Malabar, India, for whom the Archbishop of Canterbury had been a guest preacher recently. The evidence of Christianity in other cultures, where other religions are a clear majority, brought to this Conference glimpses of new challenges and different priorities and concerns. The Conference was to hear from one of the bishops of the Church of Pakistan about evangelism in Asia; a tall and powerful figure in white, Bishop Bashir Jiwan certainly came to Canterbury with a tale to tell — and something of a rebuke to issue to some of the Churches in the West, with their at times hybrid theology and seemingly indulgent speculations into dogmatics and moral theology.

'I hear some people here [at Canterbury] do not believe in the bodily resurrection of Jesus Christ', he was to say, addressing the assembled bishops in the second week, with Bishop Jenkins of Durham conspicuously seated only a few feet away on the platform. 'Without His uniqueness we have no mission or evangelism'; remarks which were received with applause. 'The Lord is doing great things in Asia' was the tale that he and many of his colleagues from Asia had come to Canterbury to relate.

Then came some of the bishops from those dioceses which have not yet been formed into a Province of their own: Bermuda, Cuba, Costa Rica, Puerto Rico, Venezuela; dioceses in Europe (Gibraltar); the Convocation of American Churches in Europe; the Lusitanian Church and the Spanish Reformed Church. Bishop Cornelius Wilson from the Diocese of Costa Rica, for example, was very clear about the agenda that he and his small diocese of only 5,000 wanted to bring to Lambeth. With just fourteen clergy and set in a predominantly Roman Catholic population estimated at over two million, what does an Anglican bishop have to say? 'Evangelism and rebuilding society' were his primary concerns: 'We have a lot of social work and we're getting participation within the Church so that the congregations will work in society and not just meet for worship.'

Anglicans Not Angels

And then with banners at the front, the bishops from each of the twenty-eight Provinces came into view, ranked in alphabetical order, their Primate detached and walking at the end of this huge procession behind the Archbishop of Canterbury, who had yet to come into sight. Traditional Anglican choir dress — scarlet chimere and white rochet — must surely be the envy of many other Churches. Nearly all the bishops were so attired. Here they came, with all their tales to tell once the service was over and they were back at the university.

Australia was first, with some thirty bishops. Anglicanism came to Australia with the first fleet of convicts and their guards in 1788, and became an independent Province in 1962. The service at St Paul's Cathedral during this Lambeth Conference marked the two hundredth anniversary of those events of 1788. The Anglican Church in Australia is large by most standards (3.7 million) with some strong leadership which emerged at the Conference in the person of Archbishop John Grindrod, who is Primate, and Archbishop Keith Rayner who was chairman of the section studying Dogmatic and Pastoral Concerns.

Immediately behind Australia came the Church of Brazil with its seven bishops, one of whom is Japanese by birth. Then the four bishops from the Church in Burma: at the end of the Conference they returned to a situation of rioting and civil war. They come from a country where the population is 87% Buddhist. In 1961 Buddhism was declared the state religion, and five years later all foreign missionaries were forced to leave. Nevertheless, on its own resources and under many difficulties, the Church has grown steadily and there are today just over 40,000 Anglicans in Burma.

Then came the French-speaking Churches of the Province of Burundi, Rwanda and Zaire. Its ten bishops including the archbishop brought to this Conference a story of courageous and heroic mission work, initiated by a neighbouring Ugandan evangelist, Apolo Kivebulayo, who at the turn of the century crossed snow-capped mountains to preach to the people of the Ituri rain-forests in Boga Zaire. Today there are nearly 700,000 Anglicans in this Province.

The Canadian bishops, some thirty-four in all, including their Primate, Michael Peers, were followed by the bishops of the Church of the Province of Central Africa founded in 1955. Led by Archbishop Khotso Makhulu, the Church here, as in the rest of Africa, had a pressing agenda which it wished to bring to Lambeth '88. Again it is a tale of lively faith, courageous witness and zealous mission and evangelism in an area of the world where there are pressing needs within the society which the Church seeks to serve. (Incidentally, along with Bishop Ting of China and and the Primate of Canada, Michael Peers, Archbishop Khotso Makhulu was awarded an honorary degree of Doctor of Divinity by the University of Kent just two days before the Lambeth Conference began.)

Two bishops represented the Church in Ceylon, each from different religious backgrounds — one Hindu, one Buddhist. In a country experiencing religious and civil strife, the minority Christian Church plays a healing role between two parties, the Tamils and the Sinhalese.

Pending the establishment of the new Provinces, the Council of the Churches of East Asia was next in the procession represented by eight bishops in all, from the Episcopal Church in Korea, Hong Kong and Macao, Taiwan, Singapore, West Malaysia, Kuching and Sabah. The Christian Churches comprise a small but growing segment of the population in most of these countries and they came to Canterbury with a passion for evangelism, a deep commitment to the faith of the scriptures, and something of an impatience with the Church in the West. It is not insignificant that the Anglican Consultative Council held its latest meeting (ACC-7) in Singapore as guest of the local bishop — Bishop Moses Tay.

The second-largest contingent of bishops came of course from England and they were next in procession. Drawn from the two Provinces of York and Canterbury, the English Church is the Mother Church of the Anglican Communion. Uniquely established by law it is totally unrepresentative of the rest of Anglicanism. In many ways it is a tired Church, not a little weary of well-doing, with not much to show for its labours and a declining membership since the Second World War. Floundering, and not unlike the English Labour party in at least one respect, the Church of England has not enjoyed a good press. The thinly veiled opposition and hostility of the English media to the Established Church was to show markedly during Lambeth '88. This stage of the procession included the Bishop of Durham, whose remarks about the Resurrection and the Virgin Birth have won him a worldwide, if somewhat unfavourable press. At the back came Bishop Graham Leonard, the principal antagonist in the endless debate about the ordination of women, who immediately before and during Lambeth '88 appeared constantly in the newspapers and on the radio and television. These bishops and many of their English colleagues came to Lambeth fatigued by tedious ecclesiastical concerns.

In quite a different style, immediately behind the English bishops, came the bishops from the Province of the Indian Ocean — Madagascar, Mauritius, and the Seychelles. There were five bishops in all, together with Archbishop French Chang-Him who was shortly to lead the congregation in the preparation for the Eucharist.

Eleven bishops from the Church of Ireland next came into view, with their distinguished and scholarly Archbishop, Robert Eames, well out of sight at the back of the procession along with the other Primates. With dioceses in Armagh, Belfast and Londonderry, these men came to Lambeth with the tyranny of terrorism on their hearts. Nevertheless, the Church of Ireland in recent years has had a fair share of renewal and it too came to Canterbury with a tale to tell and a song to sing. The surprise of the Gospel is its recurring ability to throw up good news from those very areas of the world where secular eyes discern only bad news.

Then came all the bishops from the Holy Catholic Church in Japan (Nippon Sei Ko Kai) present for the first time at Lambeth. Their Primate accompanied the Archbishop of Canterbury and stood on the Archbishop's immediate left for the Eucharistic celebration in the cathedral. The Anglican Church in Japan has 60,000 members and has just celebrated its first centenary.

The bishops from the Province of Jerusalem and the Middle East, together with their President Bishop, Samir Kafity, come from countries where Islam is all-powerful and where the focus of international politics was at its most intense during the days of Lambeth '88. What on earth can it mean to be an Anglican in Israel, Libya or Iran for example — let alone a Christian? (A face conspicuously absent from Lambeth '88 was of course that of Terry Waite.) In the twelve countries of this Province there are just 30,000 Anglicans. It was hard to know if any of these bishops had any real expectations of fruitful discussion issuing out of Lambeth for them and their fragile Church. Little wonder that the synod of this Province spoke, in January 1987, of the prospect of the consecration of a woman to the episcopate as 'at best, inopportune'. It was impossible for many of the bishops who felt as Bishop Samir Kafity and his bishops felt not to notice a group of Australian women with a large banner demonstrating in favour of the ordination of women just where the procession entered the cathedral. Happily, the 'demonstration' was markedly good-humoured and reserved.

Bishop Henry Okullu and Bishop David Gitari were among the dozen bishops present from the Church of the Province of Kenya. They came to Canterbury, along with the other African bishops, determined to tell their tales and to call their Anglican brother-bishops to a totally different agenda of priorities. As we shall see as this Conference unfolds, it was the black voice and the voices from Asia which called the rest of the Communion to repentance, to second thoughts and a different way of seeing things.

Five bishops from the Province of Melanesia, founded as an autonomous province in 1975, represent some 88,000 Anglicans from the Solomon Islands, Vanuatu and New Caledonia. At this point in the procession a Canterbury cat (possibly one of T.S. Eliot's?) fell into line behind the Melanesian banner and walked solemnly towards the cathedral — clearly aware of the auspicious occasion in which it was taking part. Eleven bishops from New Zealand followed next in the procession. Racial discussions are currently more apparent in that country, in spite of or perhaps because of the Church's commitment to equal partnership and bicultural development. The Church in New Zealand (again very small in numbers — 200,000) has gone ahead with and is strongly in favour of, the ordination of women.

Established as a Province in 1979, the Church of the Province of Nigeria is very typical of the Church in Africa. With almost 4 million Anglicans spread throughout nearly every part of that large country, the Anglican Church is the largest Christian body after the Roman Catholic Church, and is growing daily. All this, in the face of a large and militant Muslim population (45%) and in the face of poverty and political unrest. Bishop Titus Ogbonyomi of Kaduna, Nigeria, who addressed the Lambeth Conference at the plenary session called to consider African concerns, spoke of Muslim fundamentalism which had run amok, burning down churches and houses belonging to Christians in his diocese.

The Church of the Province of Papua New Guinea was followed by the banner of the Episcopal Church in Scotland. There are only 60,000 Anglicans in Scotland. Bishop Richard Holloway, the well known Bishop of Edinburgh, conspicuous for his many books and frequent appearances on television, came to the Conference with the burden of AIDS high on his agenda in the light of the many victims of the disease living in his diocese.

The next banner heralded the arrival of the twenty bishops from the Province of Southern Africa. In spite of the tensions and vicious political policies enforced in the countries from which they came, these men seemed remarkably fresh and were clearly glad to be here. Later, their Primate, Archbishop Desmond Tutu, stopped to greet them warmly as the procession of Primates filed past them on its way to the Chair of Augustine. Archbishop Tutu, Nobel Prize winner and an international figure, needed no introduction to the Conference. Anglicanism clearly has its world-figure in him — yet his face can explode at any moment into infectious laughter and mischievous humour. Presumably because he lost the official badge which all participants wore throughout the Conference, he delighted in wearing a badge which had just one word on it: 'Volunteer!' Some volunteer!

Immediately behind the Southern African contingent came the four bishops from the newest Province, that of the Southern Cone of America. The story of the South American Missionary Society which started with work among the Indians is impressive, and after just over a century Anglicans number some 27,000 in South America.

Bishop Colin Bazley of Chile made a bold claim for the Church of the Southern Cone:

> 'People are glad to be called Anglican and to be part of a Reformed Catholic Church which uses liturgy imaginatively and is continually reaching out to many thousands of people who are lost either in their poverty or else in the misery of unstewarded wealth.'

He came to Lambeth with a challenge for a 'fresh outreach in mission'.

He hoped to leave Lambeth, he claimed, with a burning passion for Christ and the Gospel, 'which would make his diocese even more proud to be Anglican.'

The Episcopal Church of Sudan's eight bishops arrived from a country where there is mounting tension beween Christians and Muslims. Bishop Daniel Zindo was later to address the Conference and tell his sad tale of the growing political power of fundamentalist Islam in his country. He challenged the Conference when telling them of the brave witness of the Sudan Churches in seeking to appeal against the reintroduction of the *Sharia* (Islamic law). He appealed to the assembled bishops for their prayers for the ending of the five year civil war in southern Sudan, where many lives have been lost and where the Sudanese people's liberation movement fights with government troops for fairer representation in parliament and for a more just distribution of resources; a tragic situation only exacerbated by the disastrous floods which greeted the bishops on their return home.

The dozen or so bishops from the Province of Tanzania which was founded in 1970 were next in line. At the charismatic conference at Canterbury the previous week, one of the bishops from this Province, the Bishop of Central Tanganyika, Bishop Madinda, related that there had been a new congregation established in his diocese every week for the past fifteen years. Muslims form 32% of the population of Tanzania and 1 million of the 8 million Christians are Anglican.

The Church in Uganda with its twenty dioceses brought tales of heroic witness under oppressive regimes to this Lambeth Conference as it had to the last Conference in '78. Only a year before Lambeth '78, Archbishop Janani Luwum had been tortured and murdered by the tyrant, Idi Amin. More than a quarter of all the Christians in Uganda are Anglican and there are almost as many Anglicans in Uganda as there are in the Episcopal Church of the United States (ECUSA).

Hot (it was very hot in Detroit) from the House of Bishops, from which a handful had slipped away early for the experience of crossing the Atlantic on the Queen Elizabeth II, came some 125 bishops from the 9 provinces of ECUSA. Sadly, the record of the Episcopal Church in the United States is a record of falling numbers. From nearly 5 million members twenty-five years ago, membership has halved and reached, along with the Church of England, an all-time low. The only signs of growth (which are considerable) are to be found (as in England) in pockets of renewal. Bishop Jack Spong of Newark, an affable and thoughtful man, was to find himself in open combat with the Bishop of London, Graham Leonard, at the Conference. Ranged as they were in opposing corners, the English press delighted in featuring them almost too prominently throughout the Conference; for Bishop Spong does not represent the whole story and he spoke very little in the plenary sessions. The Episcopal Church has been conspicuous in the past for fine missionary and evangelistic bishops who, with the Prayer Book in one hand and the Bible in the other, epitomized the frontier mentality in the name of the Gospel of Jesus Christ. Today too there are bishops who are in the front line of renewal and mission in the United States. Bishop Swing of California has ministered and witnessed bravely in the AIDS community in San Francisco. Bishop Alden Hathaway from Pittsburgh has drawn around himself a diocese of renewal ministries in the face of the declining economy of Pittsburgh. He came to Lambeth impatient to address mission and evangelism. 'The desire to present the living Christ Jesus to a torn and disbelieving world', was his agenda. 'Can there be', he asked, 'a more pressing matter before the world?' For there is Gospel power in the Church in America alongside the strange obsession with self-destruction. Together with the English bishops, the American bishops have in the past tended to dominate the plenary sessions in debate. This was nothing like so marked at Lambeth '88. Both the American and English bishops came to Lambeth '88 more ready to listen as well as to make their important contributions.

Six bishops from the tiny Church of Wales, followed immediately behind the Episcopal Church of the USA. Then, after an interlude of mainly white faces, we came back again to the black bishops, this time from West Africa, represented by ten bishops including the familiar face of Archbishop George Browne of Liberia. They in turn were followed by the bishops from the Province of the West Indies.

Word and Worship

The Primates now came into view, led by the Archbishop of Canterbury. The rain held off a little as Dr Runcie in his cope and mitre turned the corner from the old palace. Carrying his pastoral staff and preceded by the Chaplain to the Conference, Bishop Alastair Haggart, and the Assistant Chaplain, Mother Janet of the Whitby Sisters, Dr Runcie was clearly the man of the moment. Just in front of the Archbishop was Canon Samuel Van Culin, who as Secretary General of the ACC was very much an architect of this Conference. Members of the Conference were throughout unanimous in their agreement that Lambeth '88 was the best organized of any Lambeth thus far. Together with his team at the ACC, Canon Van Culin should probably pick up the prize for this accolade.

For Archbishop Runcie, all his travels in the past eight years around the Anglican Communion had finally led to Canterbury and to this opening act of worship. Behind him came Archbishop Manasses Kuria of Kenya and the Most Revd Ichiro Kikawada, Primate of Japan — both in copes. Dr Runcie first stopped to greet a child, eager to see the Archbishop in his 'party clothes' as she stood, captivated, at the front of the crowd. Then on through the great West Doors of Becket's cathedral. Inside, together with the Dean and Chapter who waited to great him, Archbishop Runcie and the congregation took up the opening hymn, 'All Creatures of our God and King'.

The great cathedral, under the brilliant lighting of the television cameras and with the splendid colours of the bishops' attire, looked as magnificent as it had probably ever looked in its long history. The Gothic arches which mark out and enclose this lofty space have observed over the centuries the Church in all its magnificence as well as the Church in turmoil, division and decadence.

The Archbishop stood flanked by the Primates as the opening act of worship for the Conference began; 'worship, the single most important part of this Conference', in the words of Bishop Haggart, the Chaplain to the Conference. The opening collect ended, the confession of sin, absolution and 'Gloria' followed. Then the ministry of the Word with the Epistle read by the Venerable Yong Ping Chung, Chairman of the ACC, and the Gospel read by Bishop Adrián Cáceres from Ecuador, culminating in the sermon. This was given from in front of the chair of St Augustine, with Dr Runcie addressing the huge congregation from a simple lecture stand, and beginning with his typically modest invocation: 'May I speak in the name of God, Father, Son and Holy Spirit. Amen.' After welcoming his fellow bishops and their wives he went on to speak openly and directly to the tensions and struggles which characterized the Anglican Communion at the outset of its deliberations at Lambeth '88.

Independence and Interdependence

Speaking of tensions within the Anglican Communion, the Archbishop in his opening sermon employed a telling analogy:

> 'As you enter this cathedral, your eye is caught by its massive pillars. In their strength they seem to stand on their own feet, symbols of strong foundations and sturdy independence. Yet their strength is an illusion. Look up and you see the pillars converting into arches which are upheld, not by independence, but through interdependence. "An arch", wrote Leonardo da Vinci, "is nothing else than a strength caused by two weaknesses; for the arch in buildings is made up of two segments of a circle, and each of these segments being in itself very weak desires to fall, and as one withstands the downfall of the other, the two weaknesses are converted into a single strength." '

A bird's eye view of the opening service at Lambeth '88

Then the Archbishop called upon the Conference to be bold and strong in the strength which God alone can supply, a strength arising from interdependence rather than independence.

'That temptation to postpone difficult decisions which we ourselves know so well does not receive much support in the New Testament record. The boldness of the present moment does often seem to be a good part of our obedience to the Holy Spirit, and if we retreat from it we should not be surprized if there is a dimming of the vision which we once had. Yet at the same time this urgency has nothing of frantic insecurity about it; it is born not of fear, but of faith. .... A Church will never learn from its mistakes unless it is ready to risk making some.'

Undoubtedly there were to be tensions, and plenty of them, as well as disagreements at the Conference which followed this service. But then as Professor Owen Chadwick reminded the Conference in his presentation during the first week:

'If there isn't any tension, it means the thing must be trivial or could be settled, as Michael Ramsey once said, by sending each other picture postcards!'

Then in conclusion, Dr Runcie went on:

'Important though this Conference is,' crucial though it may seem to the well-being of the Anglican Communion, nevertheless in the range of God's purpose it is no more than a small ship sailing on a wide, a very wide ocean. We must guide that ship as best we can. But in the end its destination and that of our Communion will not be determined by our skill and diligence as navigators, but by the power of that all-sustaining, all-embracing, ever-flowing and ever-gracious purpose of God in this, His beloved world. And to that same God, be glory in the Church by Christ Jesus throughout all ages; world without end. Amen.'

CHAPTER TWO

Witnessing to the Gospel of Reconciliation

'We need to recognize the persistence and place of conflict in Christian history. . . . We are not here to avoid conflict, but to redeem it. At the heart of our faith is a cross and not, as in some religions, an eternal calm.'
Archbishop Robert Runcie

Setting the Stage

There was certainly no excuse for getting lost — at least not geographically. Whichever way you entered Canterbury, you were greeted with bright yellow AA road signs, clearly indicating 'Lambeth Conference'. Furthermore, you could not accuse the Automobile Association of male chauvinism, for there — for all to see — were also equally bright yellow signs indicating 'Wives' Conference'.

So follow the signs — like all good pilgrims — and take the A290 out of Canterbury for a mile or so and there on top of a hill is Kent University, with its spacious residential campus affording one of the most beautiful views of the great cathedral in the walled city below. The vast Sports Hall had undergone an imaginative conversion at a cost of approximately £78,000. Canvas and carpeting covered the wooden floor, while the walls were panelled in shades of blue. At the back of the hall there was a large press gallery with ample space for television and video teams. At the front was a large stage with a huge table which could also act as the Lord's Table at celebrations of the Eucharist. A podium for principal speakers on the left of the stage and an electric organ to the right (together with a piano) supplied all the necessary props for the plenary sessions. Translation and amplification facilities, together with good stage lighting, all made for excellent conference conditions. The proceedings of the plenary sessions were sent televised around the campus to halls of residence, the communications building, the Cornwallis lecture theatre and, of course, to the BBC caravan.

The stage was set and ready as the Conference formally got under way on Monday, 18th July, with the Daily Office and Eucharist at 7:15 a.m. The first two weeks of the plenary sessions were not given over to debating but to discussions and the framing of resolutions, carried out largely away from the curious eyes and ears of the media. It was the day in London at St Paul's Cathedral and the Royal Garden Party which seemed to be the turning point of the three weeks. Up to that point the Conference appeared, at least to an observer, to be largely passive, listening to lengthy presentations and somewhat over-concerned with the one issue which, in spite of all protests to the contrary, necessarily dominated the first part of the Conference: the ordination of women to the episcopate.

Alongside all this and certainly given a higher profile than at any previous gathering of the Lambeth Fathers were the Lambeth Mothers — the Wives' Conference. Each day of the conference the wives met in St Edmund's Church of England School. There were 35 workshops on offer for the participants of the Wives' Conference. Most in demand was the one on stress, for which more than 60 wives signed up with or without, presumably, the knowledge of their husbands. Other popular workshops ranged from 'Flower Arranging' to 'Living with the Dying', 'Pottery' and 'Music in Worship'.

Yet there was an underlying seriousness to the Wives' Conference. Substantial presentations were made by Canon Colin Semper, formerly from the BBC, who spoke on Communications and Bishop Frey of Colorado who admittedly confessed that before he addressed the bishops' wives on the role of the bishop's wife, his fellow bishops had good-naturedly advised him that it 'was the dumbest thing any bishop could do' and had sent him off with 'prayers and meditations'. Later in the conference, Dean Peter Baelz of Durham spoke to the bishops' wives on 'In Vitro Fertilization: the Moral and Ethical Implications'. The theme of the first week was 'The Family in Today's World', and the theme of the second week (while debates were fermenting on the other side of the campus on women's ordination) 'Women in Today's Church'. During the second week a group of bishops' wives led by Anne Booth-Clibborn delivered a petition to Mrs

Thatcher at 10 Downing Street, not to share their insights on the stress of spouses (that might have been better addressed to Dennis Thatcher), but rather to urge her to 'sit down, and talk with those who represent the majority of South Africa'. Mrs Leah Tutu was amongst the group who delivered the petition, which had arisen directly out of the discussions and workshops of the Wives' Conference. They wished to emphasize that the South African system of apartheid takes a heavy toll on the women and children who are victims of 'appalling repression and violence'.

Since the wives were not plagued with the time-constraints imposed by the necessity of producing endless resolutions or pastoral letters, yet were without the benefit of translators, the main fruits of their conference were the strengthening of bonds of friendship in the wider family of the Anglican Communion.

Meanwhile, in the meeting rooms, corridors and pathways connecting the campus, the bishops were busy weaving the fabric of their conference, which inevitably fell under some sort of constraint because they were under pressure to have something to show by the end of the three weeks. The Steering Committee responsible for the day-to-day work of the Conference, chaired by the Archbishop of Canterbury, chose to meet each evening at 10:00 p.m. and frequently went on until after midnight. Canon Van Culin was Secretary of that group and also of the Resolutions Committee. Yet amazingly, as Secretary of the whole Conference as well, he sat on the platform attentive and lively throughout all its plenary sessions, volunteering information on housekeeping arrangements, giving guidance and gently helping the various chairmen in matters of procedure — and always with good humour.

'The Nature of the Unity We Seek'

On Monday 18th June, after a day in sections, the Conference assembled in the evening for its first major plenary session, held in the handsome Sports Hall, where it waited to be addressed by the President of the Conference, the Archbishop of Canterbury. This address was to set the mood of the Conference by tackling head-on the main concern facing the Anglican Communion at Lambeth '88. Could it stay together, and more important still, could it be an icon of unity which would facilitate further adventures in ecumenism with other Churches? Yet (perhaps even more important) could a communion of such diverse Churches display to a fragmented world in conflict something of the unity and reconciliation so desperately needed in a world which holds within its grasp the power for self-destruction and annihilation?

For what was quite clear at the outset of Lambeth '88 was that the Anglican Communion had itself developed in recent years a new capacity to self-destruct. 'There are real and serious threats to our unity and communion and I do not underestimate them', confessed the Archbishop.

> 'Some of them are the result of Gospel insights: for example the proper dignity of women in a Christian society. I hope it won't dominate this Conference, but we need to recognize that our unity is threatened over the ordination of women to the priesthood and episcopate in whatever we ultimately decide to do. There are dangers to our communion in this Lambeth Conference endorsing or failing to endorse such developments. And there are equal dangers to communion by trying to avoid the issue altogether.'

Yet Lambeth '88 had not been convened 'to avoid conflict, but to redeem it'.

At this point Archbishop Runcie referred to the advantages to be derived from solidarity between the independent Churches, not least in those parts of the world where individual Churches were involved in political confrontation. Surely, he pleaded, 'in places like the Province of Southern Africa' a solidarity within a worldwide Communion was something to be highly prized. We could do things together which we could not do individually. 'We still need the Anglican Communion', the Archbishop volunteered, 'but we have reached the stage in the growth of the Communion', he contended,

> 'when we must begin to make radical choices or growth will imperceptibly turn to decay. I believe the choice between independence and interdependence . . . is quite simply the choice between unity or gradual fragmentation. It would be a gentle, even genteel fragmentation. That much of Englishness still remains. Nor would it be instant. As I have said, the Communion is not about to disappear tomorrow. But decisive choice is before us. Do

we want the Anglican Communion? And if we do, what are we going to do about it?'

In going on to examine the nature of the unity we seek ecumenically, the Archbishop brought the discussion to a similar climax.

'As with the Anglican Communion, so ecumenically: we must move from independence to interdependence. And the same question necessarily arises: "Do we want unity?"... I do,'

he continued,

'because neither conflicting Churches nor competitive Churches nor coexisting Churches will be able to embody effectively the Gospel of reconciliation while the Churches themselves remain unreconciled. Do we Anglicans really want unity? We must do if we are to be instruments of unity and communion to a divided world.'

As the Archbishop returned to his seat on the platform the whole Conference immediately and without hesitation rose to its feet in lengthy and loud applause. The tone for the three weeks was set. From that moment there was no doubt that Archbishop Robert Runcie had taken hold, lovingly, humbly yet firmly, of the reins of the worldwide Anglican Communion in a way which would mark him out in history. The overall agenda was clear: unity in the Anglican Communion, for the sake of the wider unity of all Churches and ultimately for the sake of the world. Nothing less than that must be our agenda.

Ecumenical Relations

The following day the Conference had a somewhat longer timetable of plenary sessions in order to hear the response to the Archbishop's keynote address on unity. Representatives of the World Council of Churches and three Christian traditions, Eastern Orthodox, Roman Catholic and Reformed, were assembled on the platform of the plenary hall to make their responses. 'Generally affirmative', reported the *Lambeth Daily*, '. . . the speakers added caution and important emphases from their vantage points.'

The Revd Dr Emilio Castro was due to open the batting as General Secretary of the World Council of Churches, but unfortunately and unexpectedly had to leave the Conference to fly to Uruguay to his mother who was seriously ill. The response, therefore, for the World Council, was given by John Pobee, associate director of the WCC Programme on Theological Education, and also incidentally a member of ARCIC II. His telling response to the Archbishop's emphasis upon the need for interdependence and accountability was to point out that while we should always be 'accountable', we should nevertheless 'not be hostage one to another'. What was required ecumenically he contested was rather that we should not 'blame each other', or 'separate from each other'.

Metropolitan John Zizioulas of Pergamos gave the second response. He was 'anxious to see that the unity of the Anglican Church' was 'maintained at all costs', while conceding that it was not for him 'to say ... how to do this'. He did not dance around the unmentionable issue, for after all it was 'no secret that the Orthodox are officially opposed to any decision of the Anglicans to ordain women to the priesthood, let alone to the episcopate.' However he offered a challenge when he suggested that in his view neither the supporters nor the opponents of the ordination of women have

'even begun to treat the issue ... as a theological problem. Those opposing it have so far produced only reasons amounting to traditional practice, while those who support it often appear to be motivated by sociological concerns.'

That afternoon, the Sports Hall was not as full as might have been expected as the Conference waited to hear the response from that veteran Vatican ecumenist, Father Pierre Duprey from the Vatican Secretariat for Promoting Christian Unity. Father Duprey pointed sharply to the increasing risk that the mind of Christians, whatever their role in the Church, was today 'being formed by television, radio and the press, rather than by ... the Word of God which is heard and celebrated in the Church.'

Archbishop Runcie in his address had referred rather tentatively to the role of some kind of Petrine office, inviting all Christians 'to reconsider the kind of primacy exercized within the early Church, a "presiding in love" for the sake of the unity of the Churches.'

'The question of the nature of the unity we seek presses us to ask,' concluded Father Duprey, "What are the organs that maintain and deepen unity?" What indeed? What are the 'structures of grace' called for by Bishop Browning in the concluding sermon of the Conference? 'In recent years,' Father Duprey noted 'the Anglican Communion has paid serious attention to this and it is in terms of this concern,' he added perceptively, 'that I see the significance of the Anglican Consultative Council, the meeting of the Primates, and the developing role of the Archbishop of Canterbury.' Prior to introducing Father Duprey, Archbishop Runcie had read out a letter from His Holiness, Pope John Paul II. 'There can be no doubt,' said the Pope, 'that the ecumenical movement is a grace of God for our times, and we must thank God for the wonders He has already worked in this connection. At the same time,' he continued,

> 'conscious of the difficulties which prevent us from reaching that full communion for which Our Lord prayed and anxious lest new obstacles arise, we likewise pray to be ever more faithful to this grace, so that the works of the Lord may be fulfilled in us.'

Rather surprisingly, the Pope's message was received in silence — a silence only broken by somewhat self-conscious laughter when Archbishop Runcie referred to the 'tactful way' in which the Pope had alluded to 'known problems'.

Mrs Elizabeth Templeton, formerly a member of the Divinity Faculty of Edinburgh University, completed the responses with a skittish introduction describing herself as 'a kind of cut price, bargain specimen of those who are mostly not here — female, lay, presbyterian and … post war.' She reminded the bishops that they as bishops constituted no small stumbling block in ecumenism.

> 'It was partly because at some key points in history prelates were so unconvincing as custodians of the Gospel, that the so-called Protestants thought it best to risk God without bishops, rather than bishops without God.'

She hoped, she said, that 'the women's ordination issue' would not become 'a scapegoat for all the questions that potentially divide' Anglicans within the Anglican Communion, though, she conceded, 'it may be a focus of them'.

Throughout the early days of the Conference, Lambeth '88 received warm greetings and the promise of prayers from various leaders of the Churches right across the ecumenical spectrum. Ecumenical presence at the Conference had in fact reached an all-time high and one of the four sections of the Conference was given over entirely to the question of ecumenical relations. This section was chaired by the Primate of Canada, Michael Peers. The vice chairman was Bishop Edward Buckle from New Zealand. There were fifteen resolutions in all coming before Lambeth '88 reflecting the extensive achievements on all fronts of ecumenism in relations with a wide range of Christian Churches in the ten years since Lambeth '78 — hardly a case of 'ecumenism in the doldrums', as Archbishop Runcie pointed out.

Before the plenary session began to receive the resolutions from the section responsible for Ecumenical Relations, Archbishop Runcie made a short presentation to introduce this whole chapter of Lambeth '88. 'As Anglicans,' he told the Conference,

> 'we need to be cautious about a partisan ecumenism which supports one dialogue rather than another. We rejoice in our Catholic and Reformed heritage. This means holding all the dialogues together, resisting the temptation to upset the very careful balance the Ecumenical Section has achieved.'

He was clearly intent upon seeing the first resolution from that section, the famous *Baptism, Eucharist and Ministry Report* (fondly referred to as BEM) of the Faith and Order Commission of the World Council of Churches, as 'a convenient framework for all our ecumenical conversation. If we strongly affirm this multilateral agreement,' he continued,

> 'we can go on with confidence to vote positively for all the particular conversations in which we are engaged without being afraid that a vote for the Reformed dialogue moves us away from the Orthodox or that a vote for ARCIC separates us from the Lutherans.'

And vote with confidence and strong affirmation they did.

The *Baptism, Eucharist and Ministry Report* was strongly welcomed at Lambeth '88, 'as a contribution of great significance in the search for the visible unity of the Church.' In it, there is 'a convergence towards substantial agreement in faith and practice between many Communions.' It was against this backdrop that all fifteen ecumenical resolutions coming to Lambeth were so warmly and swiftly received.

When Bishop Edward Buckle introduced BEM, he said of the

multilateral document, 'We can no longer look out and see other confessions as satellites. We are all satellites.' The Conference then unanimously adopted a resolution praising BEM and urged its 'reception' (the process over a period of time of being 'owned' and recognized or rejected by all the Churches).

Regarding the Anglican–Lutheran dialogue, which has gone further than any of the Communion's other bilateral conversations, the Conference unanimously adopted a resolution welcoming the *Niagara Report*, released a few weeks before Lambeth, outlining specific steps to be taken toward full communion, setting up an Anglican-Lutheran International Commission and providing for 'interim eucharistic sharing'.

The Lambeth Conference unanimously adopted resolutions welcoming the new relationships being formed with the Eastern and Oriental Orthodox Churches, encouraging further conversations and suggesting that the *filioque* clause in the Nicene Creed be dropped in future liturgical revisions. The *filioque* clause says that the Holy Spirit proceeds from the Father 'and the Son'. The words 'and the Son' were added to the creed by the Churches in the West but not those in the East, and this contentious issue has been at the heart of long-term disagreements between the Churches of the East and the West. It would seem that at last this has been put to rest.

The resolution on the work of the first Anglican–Roman Catholic International Commission (ARCIC I) solicited the most discussion. The resolution recognized the 'Agreed Statements on Eucharistic Doctrine, Ministry and Ordination' as being in essential agreement with the faith of Anglicans. It also welcomed ARCIC's work on 'Authority in the Church' as a firm basis for the direction of the continuing dialogue on that subject. An amendment from some in the Church of England's evangelical wing seeking to insert mention of 'the continuing anxieties and conscientious convictions of many Anglicans unable to support this resolution' was overwhelmingly defeated in favour of the positive judgement that had come from the Provinces through the worldwide evaluation process of the original report. The original resolution passed with only seven against and three abstentions.

Alongside all these discussions at the highest level, there is a new emphasis in the 1980's upon what can be done at the local level: 'There must be local commitment and joint witness, both to the Gospel and to the values of the Kingdom', Archbishop Runcie stressed in opening the Ecumenical Relations Section of Lambeth '88. In other words, if it's real, it's local. This was confirmed by the tale told at Lambeth '88 by Bishop Keith Sutton of Lichfield, UK.

He spoke enthusiastically of a new local ecumenical programme planned in cooperation with the Roman Catholic Church to help the strife-ridden nation of Uganda. The Anglican and Roman Catholic Churches share the allegiance of 78% of the population and now plan 'to share the responsibility for the Christian rebuilding of that nation', explained Bishop Sutton. He and the Roman Catholic Bishop of East Anglia (officially appointed by the Vatican) have been hard at work on 'Operation Pearl', born of their concern and compassion for the deep pain and suffering of the people of Uganda.

> 'To a nation where 60% of the people are now under 15 years of age and 73% are under 25 years of age, "Operation Pearl" will send a team of young people from the Anglican Communion and the Roman Catholic Church to Uganda for a mission of healing. It brings great joy to witness this joint ecumenical effort and international evangelism.'

Probably the most telling 'local' event so far as the participants of Lambeth '88 were concerned was the the observance of the Russian Orthodox millenium on Saturday, 23rd July, the Feast of St Anthony of Kiev, at Vespers in Canterbury Cathedral. Metropolitan Anthony Bloom, no stranger either to Anglicans or to Lambeth, conducted the very moving service. Archbishop Runcie had recently been to Russia for the millenium celebration. The visit had made a huge impression upon him and in his welcome before the service he said that the unique event in Canterbury Cathedral during Lambeth was 'full of promise for a richer fellowship in the years to come.'

Mission and Ministry

It was given to the Section on Mission and Ministry, chaired by Bishop James Ottley of Panama, with Bishop David Sheppard as vice chairman, to handle one of the hot potatoes of the Lambeth Conference in Resolution 001 which came up on the first day. Of course the press not unnaturally wanted headlines and from the outset it was the issues surrounding the ordination of women which held out the best possibilities for this. On the Friday of the first week the Sports Hall was filled to capacity — as was the press gallery — for a two-hour plenary session on the ordination of women. This particular slot in the programme was not the place for a fullscale debate. Rather, five presentations were made on the general subject of the ordination of women to the priesthood and to the episcopate. This event drew enormous interest. The English Movement for the Ordination of Women (MOW) had established a programme of daily events at the Canterbury Centre near the cathedral. Yet not all the women at Lambeth were in favour of the ordination of women. Women Against the Ordination of Women (WAOW) distributed packets of materials to Lambeth participants; 'Yes to the Ministry of Women — No to Women Priests' was their succinct slogan.

In introducing the five speeches, Archbishop Runcie felt compelled to acknowledge that Anglicans were 'not yet of one mind on the matter, deep divisions exist between Provinces and within Provinces. Moreover, although our Communion has not been broken, it has been impaired', a word which was to recur with some frequency throughout the rest of the Conference.

The Primate of Canada, Michael Peers, refused from the outset to see this session as 'an occasion to argue a case'. As he said, he came, 'from a Province with twelve years experience of women in the priesthood' and so he saw it as 'primarily an occasion to testify about that experience'. 'I witness before you,' he said with some passion,

'that the ministry of women in our midst has been, is, and will be, life-giving. It will take different forms in different places and different ages. I pray that we will do, both at home and at this Conference, everything to affirm that life and nothing to deny its potential.'

The second speaker, unlike Michael Peers, had every intention of arguing the case, and this he did with remarkable theological passion, carefully pointing out that for him, the issue of women's ordination was part of a much wider agenda. For Bishop Graham Leonard and for the substantial number of bishops at the Lambeth Conference who clearly thought as he did, Anglicanism had now come to a fork in the road:

'For some of us what is at stake is the revealed nature of the Christian Gospel under which we stand to be judged.... That revelation recorded in scripture and which includes creation, is not something upon which we can draw to support our hopes and desires and which we are free to adopt or modify in each generation.'

To agree to the ordination of women is also to believe 'that the decision of God to be incarnate as a male... was of no ultimate significance.' In other words, he argued against the view that revelation was relative and could (and some would say must) be adapted to the cultural climate of each age. That 'Our Mother' could be just as appropriate for our God-language as 'Our Father' in an age and in a culture of feminism. His speech was certainly hard work to follow theologically yet politically it was very astute. By listing the contents of what for him was clearly a package deal, Bishop Leonard obviously expected to win support from evangelicals, conservative churchmen (recently shocked by the implications of Bishop Spong's radical agenda) and Africans and Asians for whom feminism in the West was of no relevance at best, or at worst, utterly abhorrent.

Leading protagonists in the Ordination of Women debate:
Bishop Samir Kafity, Bishop Graham Leonard,
Archbishop Robert Runcie, The Revd Nan Peete,
Archbishop Michael Peers

Bishop Samir Kafity, the President Bishop of the Episcopal Church in Jerusalem and the Middle East, was one of the strong personalities to emerge at Lambeth '88 and he was the next to speak. In essence he called for time and space for further debate throughout the whole Communion in line with the resolution passed by the Standing Committee of his own Province, which had opposed the 'consecration of a woman to the episcopate... until' there was 'a wider and deeper study of the theological, pastoral and ecumenical implications.' The case for such delay was cogently and powerfully argued in his presentation.

Yet, immediately following this, all such caution was swept away by the gracious presentation of the Revd Nan Peete, Consultant at Lambeth '88 and a black woman priest from ECUSA. Like Archbishop Peers, she simply wanted the Conference to reflect upon what had actually happened already, namely, that women like her — many hundreds of them — were already exercising a priestly ministry in the Anglican Communion. As she said, she stood there as 'the incarnation of what the three other speakers' had been talking about. She spoke movingly of her ministry in parishes — a ministry which was 'eucharistically centred' and at the same time 'involved in social action'. She was clearly not someone who saw her main role as embodying a cause. Rather, she won many hearts (and even minds) by relating her experiences, and it was no surprize therefore that when she finished speaking she received long and loud applause with about half the Conference standing to give her a warm ovation.

The lengthy proceedings were brought to a close by the Primate of Australia, the Most Revd John Grindrod. His task was in many ways much more matter-of-fact. The Primates had been asked to gather responses from the Provinces on women in the episcopate as long ago as March 1986, and the task of Archbishop Grindrod was to present that report. 'As we listened to the voices of the Provinces,' he told the somewhat weary bishops,

> 'we were impressed above all by the fact that both sides saw the matter as bound to the question of *koinonia*, that deep community in Christ which binds us to Him and to one another.'

So what 'should Lambeth '88 resolve?' he asked. 'It is difficult to avoid the conclusion,' he confesed,

> 'that the consecration of a woman would further impair our communion. However, we are not either 'in' communion or 'out' of

142

communion. The ordination of women to the presbyterate has shown us that. Would a continuing fellowship in faith, discipleship, mission, and a shared history and 'ethos' sustain our Anglican Communion while the open process of reception [that key word of Lambeth '88] was at work? Could we go forward trusting that reception, or indeed rejection, is the work of the Holy Spirit and not our work?'

In effect that is what Lambeth '88 did. On the last Monday of the Conference a whole day was set aside to debate Resolution 001. It is not true that Lambeth voted in favour of women bishops as so much of the media seemed to insist. The resolution went the way of reception, resolving that the Archbishop of Canterbury, in consultation with the Primates,

'should appoint a commission
(a) to provide for an examination of the relationship between Provinces of the Anglican Communion and insure that the process of reception includes continuing consultation with other Churches as well;
(b) to monitor and encourage the process of consultation within the Communion and offer further pastoral guidelines.'

The resolution clearly foresaw a degree of impairment within the Communion as inevitable: it would be something we, quite literally, had to live with.

Archbishop Runcie vacated the chair to speak briefly on the resolution, assuring the Conference that he was ready to initiate the commission requested by Lambeth '88 and that he would do everything in his power to 'maintain the interdependence and communion of our Anglican family of Churches ... I pledge myself and my office to this task whatever the difficulties.'

It is true that there was a second resolution before the Conference, moved by Archbishop Robinson of Sydney, who spoke strongly from the evangelical wing of Anglicanism. That resolution urged that the Provinces, 'while recognizing the constitutional autonomy of each Anglican Province', should nevertheless avoid 'further impairment of communion' and 'refrain from consecrating a woman bishop.' Archbishop Grindrod had considered such a position in his paper given earlier in the Conference. However, 'this would only be a realistic option', he said, if both sides 'could convince one another that they shared a common concern for communion.' 'Restraint cannot be imposed', he reminded the bishops, it can only be accepted 'willingly for the good of the ecclesial Communion.' The Archbishop of Canterbury seriously doubted in his intervention in the debate 'whether all Churches' would 'heed' such a call for self-imposed restraint.

Many African bishops and bishops from the developing countries were strongly opposed to the ordination of women to the priesthood. Bishop Pwaisiho of Malaita, Melanesia, said women's ordination was 'heart-breaking for Third World Churches.... If women's priesthood comes as a result of the movement for women's liberation, it is satanic.'

Archbishop Robinson's alternative resolution (002) was voted on by secret ballot and was defeated by 277 votes to 187. When the main resolution was put to the Conference it was adopted by 423 votes to 28, with 19 abstentions. Ironically, Bishop Graham Leonard and Bishop Spong both voted in favour — the former having indicated his support during the debate. Bishop Spong commented somewhat playfully later in the day: 'Now, when Bishop Graham Leonard and Jack Spong can vote for the same resolution, that's consensus!' Pressed further and asked how this had transpired, Bishop Spong replied: 'We did it by not addressing any of the really significant issues.' Nevertheless, the Conference heaved a sigh of relief and next day it was business as usual.

The Mission and Ministry Section had several other resolutions to put to the Conference, but none that would fascinate the media or give such relish as Resolutions 001 and 002.

The other resolutions dealt with important matters ranging from the question of training bishops to calls for a decade of evangelism in the 1990's — resolving 'to make the closing years of this millenium a "Decade of Evangelism" with a renewed and united emphasis on making Christ known to the people of His world.' (Echoes undoubtedly of the charismatic conference held in Canterbury the week before Lambeth.)

One whole evening was given over to the topic of Evangelization and Culture. Three bishops, from Pakistan, England and North Kenya, gave very differing presentations. Evangelization arose from sharpened and consistent theology for Bishop Bashir Jiwan from Hyderabad. 'We cannot live a godly, free and true life', he said, 'until we put ourselves under the authority of the Bible and the Lordship of

Christ.' Briefly, humourously and graciously, Bishop Jenkins of Durham side-stepped some implied criticisms of his theology by Bishop Jiwan and said succinctly that in secularized Britain 'the central Gospel issue is that of the true and living God against all idolatries, atheisms and indifferences.' For Bishop David Gitari, speaking last, 'one of the greatest problems' facing evangelization in his culture was the question of 'how to remove the Western cultural wrapper and let the Gospel encounter African cultures directly.'

Bishop Colin Bazley of Chile enthusiastically supported the resolution on evangelism, saying before the debate:

> 'It will call for a move from pastoral to mission orientation. If it passes it is of greater importance than the issue of the ordination of women as far as it changes the style and structure of the Church. We will not be a Church that will live for itself, but rather for the world.'

Resolution 048 called upon 'every diocese to conduct an evaluation of existing resources and ministry among its youth', while Resolution 042 was content to treat a much more important topic with a single sentence: recommending 'that Provinces and dioceses encourage, train, equip and send out lay people for evangelism and ministry.' In fact it was the (lay) Youth Representatives at Lambeth '88 who dragged off one or two of the bishops (Bishop Hare and Bishop Hathaway) to go evangelizing in Canterbury. Bishop Donald Taylor of the Virgin Islands even found himself hijacked for discussion by a group of young people in Canterbury. They were fascinated by his purple shirt and wanted to know what the Church was getting up to 'in that Conference'. Perhaps evangelization is more of a problem for the 'professionals' than for the customers.

Meanwhile, the Conference struggled to receive the many resolutions before there was too little time left to give them adequate treatment. In fairness, the spirit and content of many of these resolutions is better communicated and more likely to be 'received' (that Lambeth word again) by the Church at large through the pastoral letters which are sent out after the Conference. For the index of resolutions was long and the days of Lambeth too short to tackle all the topics. Lambeth should not be criticized for this. It was a healthy spirit at Lambeth '88 which attempted more than it could possibly achieve.

CHAPTER THREE

Discerning the Kingdom of God

> 'For Christians, such affirmation of pluralism has a special meaning. It embodies a recognition that every human culture has God's Kingdom as its horizon in creation and redemption. At the same time, it acknowledges that, in the dialogue between traditions, people's understanding of the meaning of God's Kingdom, and of the Christ who bears it, may be enhanced. Pluralism when understood in this way is a stimulus to the repentance by which believers discern and turn to God's Kingdom.'
>
> For the Sake of the Kingdom
> Inter-Anglican Theological and Doctrinal Commission

The Fourth Day

It all took place in a single afternoon, on the fourth day; a journey from the faintly ridiculous all the way to the heart of the matter. It was still only the first week, with unpredictable weather, unfamiliar surroundings and somewhat uncertain feelings. However, whatever Lambeth does or does not do — it always has its photograph. At least the bishops can then prove to their dioceses that they actually went to the Conference (at least for one day) and not just on a European gadabout!

In the beginning — there was chaos. Yet Anglicans do dress well: weak on dogmatic theology possibly, confused on moral theology maybe: but with a little last minute help from Wippells they are certainly well-dressed. The loud speaker moved throughout the chaos of colourfully attired prelates, speaking calming words of enlightenment peppered with typical Anglican humour. 'There's Bishop Jack Spong in just a cassock giving the illusion that he might have forgotten to pack the rest of his episcopal choir habit, with Bishop Bill Wantland looking like a theatrical version of a pre-Vatican II Roman prelate.' Yet, behold, from chaos came order. 'Then there was peace throughout the land,' recorded the *Lambeth Daily*, 'and joy in the kingdom, for the Anglicans had sorted themselves into order. And the loud speaker said it was good. He took six photographs. And then they all rested.'

Well not quite. An hour later, stripped down to shirt sleeves or casual attire, most of them were back in the plenary hall.

Communicating the Mystery

'The mystery must be communicated.' The phrase and the impact of this whole speech lingered long in the ears and hearts of those who came to Lambeth '88 ready to listen. Father Gustavo Gutierrez, a pastor theologian at the Catholic University of Lima, Peru, addressed one of the plenary sessions in that first part of the Conference devoted to listening and learning rather than talking or teaching. So Father Gutierrez said, quite boldly, that the place where all our efforts to speak about God must begin is silence and contemplation, for it is there that we can first learn for ourselves the awesome reality of God's free and unearned love for us. Only then comes the speaking, yet come it must in words matched by actions: 'the mystery must be communicated.' For Christian theology, one of liberation theology's founding fathers reminded Lambeth '88, is not a religious metaphysics, but a reflection on living faith. 'The Gospel does not say, "Go out into the world to do theology", but, "Go — make disciples!" '

In an impassioned speech, the liberation theologian reminded the bishops that our various efforts to 'do' the faith lead to different 'ways', different theologies. 'Theologies of liberation are only an attempt to understand the convergence between our affirmation of God and our behaviour.' So, 'what is the ultimate reason for the preferential option for the poor?' he asked. Not human compassion, nor justice, nor the goodness of the poor. 'God is the ultimate reason!' he declared. 'I am not called to be committed to the poor because they are good, but because God is good! The beatitudes are not a revelation about the poor, but about God.' Of course the media at the press conference afterwards had difficulty in hearing or understanding what Gutierrez had to say. 'I don't believe in liberation theology,' he reassured them in answering a question, 'I believe in Jesus Christ.' Asked what was the greatest failing of the Church in the Third World (perhaps expecting him to point to some theological nicety) he answered, quite simply, that any failure by the Church would be its refusal to love. Then came the inevitable questions implying that he was just a Marxist in sheep's clothing. 'We have heard slogans and caricatures about liberation theology and ignorance about social science and Marxism', he said, but reminded his questioners that he had never read in Marxism about the Holy Spirit acting in history.

What could have been a better preparation for, or context within which to frame, those endless resolutions which were increasingly to dominate the second part of the Conference than some crisp theology about the Kingdom of God?

For it would not be enough for the Lambeth Conference to meet simply in order to reform the Church nor in order to barter with different theologies. There were more radical questions facing the Lambeth Conference in 1988, and whether the media would misunderstand or deliberately seek to misrepresent them should be of no importance. 'Don't pity us', Archbishop Tutu said with humour at the last press conference,

> 'A Church is shown to advantage often when it is under attack. The Church gets "clobbered" when it stands up and speaks against certain policies. Archbishop Runcie certainly did over the Falklands. To be a Christian is often to be criticized.'

So while there was clearly an abiding mandate to 'communicate the mystery' there was also at Lambeth an increasing realization that the mystery is not easy to communicate — especially among communicators. But then that is no new problem!

Yet Archbishop Tutu himself certainly communicated the mystery through worship, fasting, meditation and vigil during a special evening halfway through the Conference. Here was no brand of new theology, but rather, as with Gutierrez, the Gospel in all its fullness moving from contemplation through passion to compassion, from silence and stillness to awareness and action. It was perhaps not surprising therefore that at some point the African bishops would speak out. When asked what and where would be the African influence at Lambeth '88, Bishop David Gitari from Kenya replied: 'In the area of peace and justice — here we will make our mind felt.' And so they did. The agenda of the Committee for African Concerns (CAC) had arisen out of the Cambridge meeting of African bishops immediately before Lambeth. The African Anglican Provinces in CAC were Burundi, Rwanda and Zaire; Central Africa; the Indian Ocean; Kenya; Nigeria; Southern Africa; Sudan; Tanzania and Uganda. A special plenary session was called on the day following the Royal Garden Party in an attempt to 'communicate the mystery' of poverty and the needs of the African countries. Their message constituted an economic and political, as well as theological, challenge to the Western nations. The session concluded with the singing of what has become an almost international anthem: 'God Bless Africa'.

Not Just a Talk Shop

At the beginning of the Conference a message was sent from Lambeth '88 to the black South African leader, Nelson Mandela, held by the South African government at Pollsmoor Prison in Capetown. The occasion was Mandela's 70th birthday and the message read quite simply:

> 'The archbishops and bishops of the Anglican Communion gathered at Canterbury for the Lambeth Conference send birthday greetings on a day when we remember you and your family in our prayers.'

The cynic might ask: 'What is achieved by this kind of thing?' Professor Owen Chadwick in his light, yet serious presentation to the Conference in that first week of listening was quite clear about his answer to that particular question. Resolutions and messages on topics of justice, peace and humanitarian concerns from successive Lambeth Conferences were more, not less important, in his view. Referring to the famine in Ethiopia which was, for example, the subject of a resolution adopted as long ago as Lambeth 1920, he said that such a resolution 'was a way of making sure that prayers were directed where they were needed'. Referring particularly to two resolutions on nuclear disarmament, one in 1948 and the other in 1958, Chadwick said,

> 'Anyone who reads what was said on that subject would be grateful that those debates occurred and will feel that, impracticable or not,

the Fathers dealt with a subject of supreme importance to humanity and, further, that something would have been missing if they
had not sought to discuss it.'

Archbishop Tutu echoed this sentiment when speaking of political
resolutions in the BBC's *Lambeth Walk*, 'They help', he said. 'Any soft-
pedalling would have caused headlines. They help create a particular
climate, help shape public opinion, help victims of oppression. It is
important for us at Lambeth not to be seen as just a "talk shop".'

It was in that spirit that the Conference invited Dr Jonathan Mann,
the Director of the World Health Organization's Global Programme
on AIDS, to address the bishops at Lambeth '88. Dr Mann noted that
AIDS was the first disease ever to be discussed in the General Assembly of the United Nations or at a world leaders' economic summit.
Surely that was a testimony to the broad impact of the disease as a
worldwide challenge. Yet he gave a message of hope, when he said,
'We know now that we will learn to dominate the disease — through
resolute commitment to interdependence.' (Significantly a word
used, though in another context, with some power and fullness of
meaning by Archbishop Runcie.) 'We will not allow the disease itself
or the fears and forces which it can unleash, to dominate us.' When
asked after his presentation on whether use of the common cup at the
Eucharist posed any risks, he commented, 'I would have no hesitation
drinking from a cup used by someone infected with the HIV virus.
The virus is rarely present in the saliva at all and never in large quan-
tities.' He concluded that no study had ever shown transmission of the
disease through saliva. There had been a moment of laughter at the
beginning of the session when Dr Mann was mistakenly referred to as
Dr Aids. Bishop William Swing of California, USA, took up this point
afterwards in a news conference.

'When a bishop can be described as "Bishop Aids", then we'll know
we're ready to start having an impact. We haven't got our act
together at all yet.'

And in a later interview he continued,

'In ten years, what human suffering and human carnage! The bishops will come limping back to Lambeth in ten years saying: "Why
did you not prepare us for the devastation?" The most important

statement on AIDS from the Church had come from Presiding Bishop Edmond Browning, ECUSA, who said, "Walk with one AIDS victim." I wish every archbishop would make a similar statement.'

With some frustration he concluded, 'There has been no time at Lambeth '88 on priests with AIDS. Believe me, its coming!' And bishops too?

Christianity and the Social Order

Dr Mann had been addressing a plenary session of the Christianity and Social Order Section of the Conference, chaired by Archbishop John Habgood of York, with Archbishop Desmond Tutu as vice chairman. It was this section which produced the largest number of resolutions for debate in the plenary session. There were some resolutions which spoke to immediate concerns in the world political arena and which needed to be well-timed if they were to achieve maximum impact. 'It's a tradition at Lambeth Conferences,' said Archbishop Runcie, 'to react immediately to issues that are important. The time is now,' he insisted, 'over the question of peace or war in the Middle East.'

So in addition to Resolution 025 on Iran already put forward by the Section on Christianity and the Social Order, an emergency resolution was rapidly put together and unanimously adopted by the Conference on Tuesday, 2nd August. Proposed by Bishop Robert Witcher of Long Island, USA, and seconded by Archbishop George Browne of West Africa, the resolution welcomed Iran's acceptance of the United Nations Security Council Resolution 598 to end the conflict in the Middle East and looked to Iraq to honour its commitment to do so; it condemned the use, sale and supply of chemical weapons; it recognized the grief and suffering of hostages, their families and all victims of the war; and asked all nations to work towards the release of all hostages in Lebanon, whatever their nationality.

It so happened that the resolution was presented the day after Archbishop David Penman of Melbourne confirmed that he had visited Iran prior to arriving at Lambeth at the request of the Archbishop of Canterbury. Archbishop Penman was mildly optimistic that Terry Waite and other hostages might be released before the end of the year.

When Resolution 025 came before the plenary sessions later in the Conference it was proposed by Bishop Dehqani Tafti, the Bishop of Iran in exile, and Assistant Bishop of Winchester since 1982. 'Real theology is always written in blood', he began.

> 'All the diocesan offices were taken by force, false claims made against bishops, and one has been detained and imprisoned in Iran for eight years. Our legal existence is threatened . . . we must stop the procrastination. . . stop the imprisonments and murders.'

This impassioned plea came from a bishop whose own son was murdered by the regime in Iran. 'Love without backbone,' he concluded, 'is "wishy-washy" and weak.'

In an equally emotional statement, the Bishop of Northern Uganda, Benoni Ogwal Abwang, gave the resolution 'strong support' and said,

> 'I too am in exile. Similar things have happened to me and my staff. I feel sorry that we cannot extend the resolution to other countries as well.'

The resolution 'respectfully' requested that the Islamic Republic of Iran would respond positively to the claims of the Church in Iran. A similar urgent resolution also relied heavily on good timing. Bishop Jim Thompson of Stepney, London, proposed Resolution 038 on Namibia ahead of time so that it would coincide with the meeting in Geneva between the United States of America, South Africa, Cuba and Angola to discuss the United Nations peace proposals for Namibia. 'A generation of Namibian children is growing up in refugee camps in Angola and Namibia', said Bishop Thompson.

> 'Young people are kidnapped and forced to join the army. Church buildings have been destroyed and the Church persecuted. So our resolution expresses our love, support and admiration for the Church in Namibia.'

The full text of this resolution, expressing support for the people of Namibia in their struggles for independence, and calling upon the South African government to withdraw from Angola, was sent with the unanimous backing of the Lambeth Conference to Geneva.

However, another timely resolution from the Section on Christianity and the Social Order, entitled 'War, Violence and Justice', ran into some difficulties. 'This Conference understands', said Resolution 027,

> 'those who, after exhausting all other ways, use the way of armed struggle as the only way to justice, while drawing attention to the danger and injustices possible in such action.'

Led by the Bishop of Clogher, Ireland, Bishop Brian Hannon, the Conference was asked to reconsider its words:

> 'This could possibly be an opening for propaganda used by the IRA. I cannot see people from any of the Irish Churches being happy with it.'

Archbishop Tutu, however, rose and spoke with persuasion on this matter from the point of view of freedom-fighters in South Africa and elsewhere. He extended the traditional thesis of 'a just war' to a 'just revolutionary situation'. 'It is crucial for us to be consistent', he claimed. 'The Church is not pacifist.... All we are saying is that we do understand when people say: "For us, this is the last resort."' So the resolution was passed without any concessions.

Coming as it did in a week of renewed sectarian violence in Northern Ireland and only days after the Mill Hill barracks bombing by the IRA, the resolution drew angry protests from British politicians. 'Bishops give backing for violence as last resort' was one headline next morning. The Irish bishops spent a sleepless night trying to frame a subsidiary resolution. As soon as the plenary session convened on Friday, and having seen the morning newspapers, Archbishop Eames of Armagh asked permission to address the Conference. He pointed out with some passion that the wording of the previous day's resolution had brought 'distress and disbelief'. 'The words, "armed struggle", have a particular connotation' in his part of the Anglican Communion, he stressed, 'as they are associated with the sophisticated propaganda of the Provisional IRA, which is engaged in a ruthless campaign of murder and destruction.' Hastily an emergency resolution was unanimously carried stating that the Conference expressed 'solidarity with fellow Anglicans and with all the people of Northern Ireland in their suffering', and that 'in the circumstances of Northern Ireland', it condemned all violence. This last explicit condemnation of all violence was inserted at the specific request of Bishop Simon Barrington Ward of Coventry, UK, whose bid for the inclusion of such an explicit clause brought loud and spontaneous applause from the Conference. Ironically, or perhaps significantly, the emergency resolution was passed at the same time as the bishops' wives marked the end of their conference by releasing balloons with the words 'Peace' and 'Hope' printed on them.

This whole episode was something of an unfortunate hiccup in Lambeth '88. Bishop Westwood of Peterborough, UK, described the original resolution on 'War, Violence and Justice', as 'armchair bravery' — even 'cheap' — and claimed that it would clearly cause real problems to people 'in the real world'. A more generous assessment is probably nearer the mark when the incident is viewed in perspective and with hindsight. Pan statements are notoriously difficult and dangerous. Ringside judgements must always be tempered by the voice which comes from where the action is. Both Archbishop Tutu and Archbishop Eames were such voices at Lambeth '88. The situation in Northern Ireland is clearly very different from that in South Africa. Robert Eames said he had seen so many blunders made by people commenting on Northern Ireland who had not done their homework, that he did not wish to fall into the same error by commenting on South Africa. 'I do not want to make the job of the Church there any harder', he said.

> 'I know and like and respect Tutu. I think he is a man of great courage and I hope some way will be found to help those in South Africa who find they are on the wrong end of injustice.'

Further resolutions from the Section on Christianity and the Social Order on matters concerning sexuality brought forth even more lively debates. Resolution 029 on AIDS was formally debated by the whole Conference. The bishops were on the whole unsympathetic and refused to make any concessions to a homosexual lifestyle — much to the righteous indignation of Bishop Paul Moore of New York, who wanted the Church to be positive and realistic about those who 'would not or could not marry'. The official motion on AIDS and a private member's motion on human rights for homosexuals were radically amended. It was the African bishops, coming from areas where AIDS is endemic, who called for amendments along more traditional lines. One African bishop said,

> 'When you speak of homosexual rights, what does that mean? You

are speaking of the rights of sin, and that I am totally against. It is
totally anti-Biblical. Leviticus says the practice is an abomination.'
'For those of us who know sin as sin,' said Archbishop Kuria, the
Primate of Kenya,

> 'and preach against it as sin: to allow and to support people who
> continue in sin, and to help them only not to be infected with the
> disease AIDS, that is not the Gospel of Jesus Christ.'

It was the African bishops along with the Western traditionalists (a
sizeable majority throughout the Conference) who were not prepared to accept anything other than Biblical morality. Bishop Paul
Moore in his private member's motion (064) on the practice of homosexuality had an even rougher ride. For him, homosexuality was a
question of human rights, the category in which he tends to place so
much. The Conference was not in the mood, however, to go down
that road and refused to go any further in its recognition of homosexuality than it had already in 1978. After the debate on AIDS Bishop
Moore strode from the platform saying, in a somewhat aggrieved
time: 'I am surprised Lambeth wishes to say that.' Moore might have
been surprised with how little Lambeth was prepared to say to help
homosexuals, but many more would have been more surprised if
Lambeth had tried to say more! Bishop Browning confided at the
final news conference that he was 'personally disappointed in the vote
on homosexuality and human rights as are many bishops in the
American Church.'

The African bishops came to Lambeth determined, after 121 years,
to have an accomodating and pastorally helpful resolution on polygamy come out of Lambeth. In reality Lambeth '88 was only being
asked, according to Bishop David Gitari, to endorse an earlier statement from an ACC meeting in Dublin in 1973 which suggested that
'in the case of conversion [into the Church], a polygamist may be
received in suitable cases.' With only scattered opposition, yet with a
notable number of abstentions, the Conference approved in principle
that under certain conditions:

> 'in cultures where polygamy is practised and socially acceptable, a
> polygamist who responds to the Gospel and who wishes to join the
> Anglican Church may be baptized and confirmed with his believ-
> ing wives and children'.

The conditions are quite specific. The polygamist must promise not to marry again whilst any of his wives at the time of his conversion are alive, while the 'local Anglican community' must approve his acceptance into the Church. All these considerations were set within the context of affirming 'monogamy as God's plan and as the ideal relationship of love between husband and wife.'

With its many resolutions, the Section for Christianity and the Social Order held the floor of the plenary sessions for lengthy and at times passionate debate. When the dust settles, and the reports are published, there will doubtless be many who will ask what on earth Lambeth was doing in concerning itself with such matters as AIDS, homosexuality, Namibia or, for that matter, Northern Ireland. Should the Church meddle in political matters? This question, particularly in recent years, has frequently been addressed to the Church of England. Yet the words of Guttierrez ring true for all the Churches' concerns, when he said, 'not because the poor [the victims of AIDS, homosexuals, Namibians, etc] are good: but because God is good.' It is the task of the Church and indeed of the Lambeth Conference, by deed and by word, never to let the world forget that fact.

'The right and duty of Christians to speak and act on problems of social order needs no defence', says the report from the Section on Christianity and the Social Order.

> 'It follows directly from our belief that this is God's world, and that He has shown His care for it in creation, incarnation and redemption, and in His promise that all things ultimately will be brought to fullness in Himself. ... No part of human life is excluded from God's care and concern. ... In all our work we are called to keep before us the vision of God and of a transformed humanity which both challenges our present experience and offers us hope in the task.'

Dogmatic and Pastoral Concerns

It was this same 'vision of God' and His Kingdom which illuminated the discussions of the Section on Dogmatic and Pastoral Concerns. This section produced only six resolutions, and was chaired by Archbishop Keith Rayner, Archbishop of Adelaide, with Bishop Mark Dyer of Bethlehem, USA, as the vice chairman. They took as the starting point for all their deliberations the historical fact that 'in the fullness of time, God sent His Son, born of a woman'. The resolutions and the subsequent report were remarkably free from both ecclesiastical neurosis or Anglican identity-questing.

In that first week of listening and learning there was one whole evening given over to the underlying question of Lambeth '88, namely the thorny question of authority. As chairman of the section, Archbishop Rayner gave the major presentation. 'For the Anglican Communion,' he said,

'the authority question has become critical. . . . The problem is sharply focused with respect to diversity of opinion on the ordination of women to the priesthood and possibly the episcopate.'

He reminded the Conference that they had 'no right to demand instant to say nothing of infallible answers to all questions in controversies of faith.' 'We have our Lord's promise that His Church will not ultimately fail,' he reassured the bishops,

'but, we have no promise that the Church or any organ of the Church, will be enabled to answer every question of faith immediately and infallibly.'

On the specific question of ordaining women as priests, Archbishop Rayner said:

'an acceptance of the authority of the Churches to decide and act.. is gradually emerging within the Anglican Communion. The reception [a word which was used increasingly at Lambeth '88] of that decision within other Communions of the Catholic Church has still a long way to go. In the meantime, the decision will still have a provisional character.'

This is the acid test of the Anglican experiment: can it live not only in diversity but provisionally content with 'only one step' visible, in an unfolding revelation of the mystery of God?

Later that evening, Professor Rowan Williams, Lady Margaret Professor of Divinity at Oxford University, confessed that there is 'no final way' of knowing whether 'what may seem a proper development in our proclamation is not a local eccentricity or a vapid fashion.' But, he added, 'there is no alternative to making a decision about [women's ordination]. . . . Neither side can claim straightforward authorization. Both are bound to what Christian adulthood requires of every believer, the readiness to act in hope.'

For equally we must remember that no decision 'is no less a decision'. So it was along the lines of a higher pragmatism that Professor Williams suggested authority in the New Testament sense was vindicated. Authority in the New Testament, both in the person of Jesus and in what he gave to his disciples, is not an abstract formula which is infallible. Rather it 'indicates the capacity to do something.' 'In short, the idea of "authority" in the Gospels is connected far more with how we do things, than with how we know things.' It is a question of living the life in order to know the doctrine.

The authority which we should look for in our Church is the power given by God alone in the war against evil to cast out devils, to heal the sick and to forgive sins. This is true authority, power (*exousia*) in the New Testament, and it is given by the Father and shared with the apostles of Christ. Professor Williams called for an element of this kind of pragmatism and for something of an adult faith during the period when the Church is in the process of receiving (or perhaps ultimately rejecting) the sort of development which would include women in the episcopal college. As in the Old Testament we simply cannot see the face of God. Only in retrospect can we see where His hand has been (or has not been) in all of this.

'Yet are there limits to diversity and where do they lie?' asked Archbishop Rayner. 'How and by whom are they determined?' The Conference did not really tackle the first question — perhaps such a large body would have been foolish to try. The second question was answered in large measure in the text of Resolution 018: 'The Anglican Communion: Identity and Authority'. The four ingredients of decision making and communication: the Archbishop of Canterbury, the Primates, Lambeth Conferences and the Anglican Consultative Council, were all somewhat upgraded. Some bishops had a higher doctrine of the latter than others, urging that a kind of pan-Anglican synod should be developed to give the ACC more scope. Happily the Conference did not endorse that. Archbishop Runcie modestly urged the Conference both in this resolution and in another to cut the office of Archbishop of Canterbury down to size to ensure that the office did not become a kind of Anglican papacy but remained *primus inter pares.* The importance of the Primates was highlighted during Lambeth by the refurbishment work being carried out in the Chapel at Lambeth Palace. Each Primate is to be allocated his own stall with the crest of the Province displayed above. In seeking to upgrade the contribution of the Primates such a move should help in the creation of a college of Primates, strengthening the structures of unity for the independent Provinces. Dr Runcie, in consultation with the Primates, moved to ensure that a specially appointed Inter-Anglican Commission was speedily set up to maintain unity and deal with the structures of the Communion which were likely to be more or less impaired by the consecration of a woman bishop. The setting up of an advisory body on Prayer Books for the Anglican Communion was also included in the resolution. One English bishop spoke of this suggestion rather disparagingly as an 'expensive white elephant'. Bishop Frank Griswold of Chicago, however, saw such a body as a doctrinal body which would guard against possible excesses of local enthusiasm. He said 'strong, central pressure' was needed to ensure that worship and liturgy remain vehicles of unity among Anglicans.

Of course the development of such structures also implies a higher budget for the Anglican Communion, which according to recent figures is already under financial pressure. In the ACC budget for 1987 there was a shortfall of £23,000. Indications are that there will be a more serious shortfall in 1988 and 1989. It is not perhaps too alarmist to say that a financial crisis, at least for the ACC, looms on the horizon. Lambeth '88 has still to put its money where its mouth was during the somewhat heady days of the Conference. Notwithstanding, the remaining resolutions were received with a minimum of debate.

One particular resolution from this section demands at least a mention, Resolution 021: 'Interfaith Dialogue: Jewish, Christian and Muslim' proposed by Bishop Richard Harries of Oxford. He was busy throughout the three weeks — giving the impression of all kinds of subterfuge. The original draft report prepared by the Bishop of Oxford was entitled, 'Jewish-Christian Guidelines for the Anglican Communion: *The Way of Dialogue*' and dealt exclusively with the two faiths. The final document that came before a somewhat weary and resolution-battered Conference included, however, that third faith which descends from Abraham and thus had the broader title 'Jews,

Christians and Muslims'. Richard Harries openly admitted that the document had passed through ten versions — no wonder he looked a little preoccupied from time to time. He was. The original document was extremely liberal in outlook, firmly rejecting 'any form of proselytizing which attempts to convert individual Jews to Christianity'. The final version of 'The Way of Dialogue' commended by Resolution 021 only rejects 'all proselytizing that is aggressive or any manipulative attempts to convert, and of course, any hint of anti-semitism'. The report states that there are many areas of common interest where the three faiths can now work together, and goes on to suggest four such areas: struggles against racism, apartheid, anti-semitism and work for human rights, particularly the right of people to practice and teach their religion.

In their final report, the section responsible for Dogmatic and Pastoral Concerns claimed that 'Anglicanism has always embraced a variety of theological opinions within a fundamental unity of faith and order.' What perhaps it did not acknowledge sufficiently is that the prospect of the ordination of women bishops in some Provinces and not in others will bring a new diversity to Anglicanism. It will not now be simply a question of a 'variety of theological opinions' but also a diversity in church order — not just faith but practices will be sharply diversified. Can we live with that?

Lambeth '88 ended leaving as many if not more questions than were there when it had first gathered. When Bishop Raymond Lessard, the Roman Catholic Bishop of Savannah, Georgia, USA — a member of ARCIC II — was asked which major issue must first be resolved before he could expect greater unity between Roman Catholics and Anglicans, he answered not surprizingly, somewhat tersely though totally affably: 'Questions of authority — who exercizes it, and through what instruments?' One suspects he left Lambeth '88 with a very Anglican answer to his very Roman Catholic question.

For on questions like that, Lambeth '88 could not hope to be more than a resting place on the long pilgrimage of faith. Christians have to learn to live provisionally, as though the kingdom has already come, and yet in the knowledge that it has not yet come, daily praying the while: 'Thy kingdom come.' So, as Professor Chadwick pointed out in his lecture on Lambeth Conferences during the first week of Lambeth '88,

'One of the funniest and yet most moving of all the episodes of Lambeth Conferences was when they went on pilgrimage to Holy Island in 1908...the organisers had mistaken the time of the tide, so bishops were ploughing ["plodging" was actually the wonderfully evocative word he used] through the sea up to the waist in order to say their prayers at so holy a sanctuary. I find that story characteristic of the Anglican Communion and also very edifying.'

And so it is. Nearly every Lambeth Conference has gone on a pilgrimage of sorts because in some sense every Lambeth Conference is itself a pilgrimage of faith. Lambeth '88 was no exception. Several of the 'holier' bishops went to Walsingham to the Shrine of our Lady and upset some Protestant protesters there. Others had a day's outing to Boulogne. Truth is notoriously illusive and is often appropriated only after you have first gone out of your way on an unknown road to a place where holy belief and prayer have rested and resided through the ages. The journey is just as important as the arrival: the process is as important as the achievement. All pilgrimages are fun, they expose you to the climate and often result in sore feet.

By 1998 the tunnel under the English channel will be complete. By then, as the adverts say, it will be possible to go from A to B without going through sea. If the next Lambeth is held in England, perhaps the Lambeth Fathers could be persuaded to get the best of both worlds — Walsingham and Boulogne — by going to that ancient monastery of Bec in France, where the food and wine are of Benedictine modest excellence; where English is spoken as well as French (for bilingual pilgrims like Michael Peers of Canada), and where the roots of Anglicanism before the Reformation are to be uncovered and experienced.

CHAPTER FOUR

Signposts at the Crossroads

'Our [Anglican] Communion is for a purpose, to look towards the Lord Jesus as He leads us into what seem impossible tasks. Some thought this Conference was impossible. Reason and experience suggested that we would fall apart. But by keeping our eyes on the Lord, it has not sunk!'
Archbishop Runcie

Farewell Anglican Communion?

Heads out of nearly every window — 'There's Bishop Hatendi from Harare and Archbishop Carnley of Perth at the same window.' The pipe band was playing 'Auld Lang Syne' as the last luggage was packed aboard the train. It was Sunday, 7th August, 1988, as at 3:03 p.m. the specially chartered Episcopal Express with several hundred bishops and their wives on board pulled out of Canterbury West Station bound for Victoria. 'Your Grace, your Grace — look out for your hat' someone shouted. Archbishop Runcie and his wife stood on the platform waving fond farewells, the former with straw hat in hand as a last relic of the ill-fated Lambeth '88 cricket match. These Canterbury pilgrims had arrived three weeks earlier under heavy clouds and foreboding skies to the rain-drenched fields of Canterbury. During those three weeks the warmth and sunshine of friendship had displaced the clouds of initial caution for the bishops and their wives. So with two blows of the whistle the train took the bishops and their luggage all the way to Victoria and from there they spread to the four corners of the world. The Lambeth Conference of 1988 was finally over.

The previous evening, the Feast of the Transfiguration, the Conference had gathered outside in bright evening sunshine to plant a tree for peace, for it was the anniversary of 6th August, 1945, when the first atomic bomb was dropped on Hiroshima. 'Make me an instrument of your peace', were the words on the lips of Ichiro Kikawada, the Primate of the Holy Catholic Church in Japan, as the extract from the ancient prayer of St Francis, amplifed by the devices of technology, rang out over the university campus. 'Make me an instrument of your peace' he said a second and yet a third time. The tree was planted. The crowd reluctantly dispersed, lingering in the late evening sunshine. At the end of the last plenary session that afternoon, Dr Runcie had urged the bishops to go back to their dioceses, 'Where I pray you will dare to do great things for God.'

'Our Conference is over', said Bishop Browning in his address in Canterbury Cathedral on the last Sunday morning.

> 'We have listened to each other. We have worshipped together. We have struggled together. We now return to our Provinces, to our dioceses, to our clergy and laity, to our families and those who support us.... We now return to ask them to pray with us to discern the will of God. To help to make together the fabric of a united Communion.... We now go out into the world, in the name of Jesus' he concluded, 'to proclaim not a new religious bureaucracy, not new religious laws, not new charts of ecclesial organization, but structures of grace.'

Structures of Grace

'Structures of grace'? Is that what Archbishop Desmond Tutu meant when, in his puckish style, he summed up the Conference and the Anglican Communion as being 'totally untidy but very, very lovable?' 'There was nothing about forcing anybody to toe a particular line,' he reflected, 'and that is a part of the ethos and genius of our Communion.' Well, is it? Certainly for those who are looking for a streamlined catholicism, the 1988 Lambeth Conference only evoked further frustration. Dr William Oddie, with predictable rancour, asked rhetorically when it was all over: 'Should the bishops agree to go their separate ways?.... The extraordinary circus ... is packing up the big top. Soon the performers...will scatter to the far corners of the earth.' And then, as a prophet of gloom and doom, he continued, 'The Anglican Communion is in for a rough passage; it is battening down the hatches and attempting to install damage-limitation equipment.' No, that is not what Bishop Browning had meant by 'structures of grace'. Certainly not for anyone attending the Conference, and least of all for those waving farewell at Canterbury West, did it feel as though they were leaving to 'batten down the hatches'. 'Anglican bishops believe in independence far more strongly than in unity', William Oddie proclaimed somewhat questionably. 'And quite simply, you cannot have them both.' Can't you?

Independence and Interdependence

The pilgrimage to maturity surely moves through three distinct phases in the life of an individual, a nation or a Church. Necessarily the journey through life begins with dependence. Such a stage is totally appropriate in infancy but wholly inappropriate and even unhealthy in adulthood. Dependence must give place to stormy episodes as independence is rightly demanded by the teenager and colonist alike. In striking out for independence, difference and identity are vigorously championed as the distinctive characteristics of the individual emerge. Fragmentation in the name of specialization becomes overwhelmingly apparent, and timorous spirits are tempted to regress to a more conventional chapter, where everything appears to be so much more straightforward and so much less complicated. Yet there is a third stage in this development which can only emerge in an environment of grace; as dependence gives place to independence, so independence is transcended by interdependence — an interdependence among peers and equals, in which the old battles are not surrendered, but are set within more generous and spacious fellowship. Interdependence is the healthy goal of all development and growth.

It was the interdependence of the twenty-eight self-governing and autocephalous Provinces which emerged out of Lambeth '88, a quality of communion which could perhaps best be experienced before it could be communicated to those not present at the Conference. Or in the snappy phrase of Bishop Jenkins of Durham, 'We agreed to belong rather than belonging in order to agree.' It was this kind of unity of fellowship 'which was perhaps the most significant thing for the

Conference', concluded the London *Times* in a surprisingly refreshing and positive leading article at the end of Lambeth '88:

> 'The participants were still facing broadly in the same direction as they reached port. They emerged as friends, still unable to agree about several key issues, but still recognizably members of the same episcopal college. When they set out three weeks ago such a result seemed unlikely.'

For there is a crisis which arises precisely from such a decision to be committed and from the refusal to permit differences to lead to fragmentation. When we fragment we flee from the pain of commitment. In some form after Lambeth '88, the Anglican Communion is more committed than ever, though its shape is admittedly more unformed and unsure. 'I thank God for what we form as a Communion', Archbishop Runcie had said in his opening sermon in the cathedral:

> 'not an Empire, nor a Federation, nor a jurisdiction, nor yet the whole Church, but a Communion — a fellowship based on our gathering at the Lord's Table, where we share "the means of grace and the hope of glory".'

Yes, that is what Bishop Browning presumably meant by 'structures of grace'.

It was in this kind of theological climate that Archbishop Runcie had bowled the first ball of Lambeth '88 in his opening address, 'The Unity We Seek':

> 'The New Testament surely speaks more in terms of interdependence than independence. The relationship of Jesus with the Father in the bond of the Holy Spirit as witnessed in St John's Gospel surely gives us the pattern of Christian relationship. Life together in communion implies basic trust and mutuality. Think of Paul speaking of life in the Body in his first letter to the Corinthians: "The eye cannot say to the hand, I have no need of you, nor again the head to the feet; I have no need of you." (1 Corinthians 12:21) Or think of Paul's collection for the saints in Jerusalem, a practical expression of communion on the theological ground of unity in Christ.'

Structures of Grace and Instruments of Unity

Archbishop Eames, who, incidentally, emerged as one of the voices and faces of Lambeth '88, had in his pre-Lambeth study produced a helpful resource document which was circulated to all members of the Conference ahead of time. Much of its content was reflected in a weighty and substantial presentation to the whole Conference on the first Friday — 22nd July. Archbishop Eames, tipped by the sweepstake of the English press as a possible successor to Dr Runcie, spoke on 'Instruments of Communion and Decision-making: the Development of the Consultative Process in the Anglican Communion'. The issues he dealt with and which faced the Fathers of Lambeth '88 did not arise however, 'simply because the Anglican Communion was in some sort of trouble' — or at least that is what Archbishop Eames insisted. They arise and will continue to arise, he argued, because the Communion has grown and 'developed as a worldwide family to a point where certain questions must be asked' if it is to grow — or else it will die. Yet growth, in the words of Archbishop Runcie, is painful for the Anglican Communion for we have 'reached a stage in growth ... when we must begin to make radical choices or growth will imperceptibly turn to decay.'

'If we belong to the club,' contended Archbishop Eames in his formal presentation, 'let us make our membership just as effective when we disapprove of each other as when we approve.'

So, as we have seen already in the chapter on Dogmatic and Pastoral Concerns, the Lambeth Fathers of '88 placed renewed emphasis upon the four instruments of Communion — the Archbishop of Canterbury, the Lambeth Conference, the meeting of the Primates and the Anglican Consultative Coucil. In addition, they moved to set up the Commission on Inter-Anglican Relations to work out the 'structures of grace' which would be needed in the event of the consecration of a woman bishop by any one of the self-governing Provinces. While it is obvious why such an action will produce particular difficulties and therefore might well require a special commission to deal with the issues in an ad hoc, urgent and practical way, one is nonetheless tempted to ask why the four-fold instruments of communion should not resolve this themselves at the outset, using the contentious issue of the ordination of women to the episcopate as a chance to strengthen the developing communication. For, presumably, in any event the commission will report to the Primates and then the process of inter-action between the four elements making for unity will be drawn upon for the continuing and far-reaching responsibility of preserving unity in diversity, and independence within interdependence. 'It is probably under such immediate pressures as this,' concluded the *Times* leader, 'that a workable and acceptable structure of leadership in the Anglican Communion will be muddled into shape.' Perhaps it was the crisis itself which led to new commitment at Lambeth '88.

Lambeth '88 in Particular and Lambeths in General

So, we might ask: 'In what ways did Lambeth '88 take its place in that shaping process?' At the cost of approximately £775,000 (which is by no means expensive by the standards of other international confer-ences), what did Lambeth achieve? In spite of the criticisms of much of the English press, the answer should be boldly pronounced that its achievements were not unimpressive. Since the outset, Lambeths have had their advocates and their detractors. Yet the chances are that when the five hundred or so bishops left Kent University most of them returned to their dioceses in a more positive frame of mind than when they had arrived, and certainly many of them were more openly enthusiastic than they had been previously about their membership of the Anglican Communion.

For Bishop Browning and for several others it was their third Lambeth, and most of them would have echoed his words when he said that of the three Conferences it was 'the best prepared for'. The 'women's issue' in retrospect had not dominated the Conference but rather had acted, claimed Bishop Browning, as 'a catalyst'. Everyone was 'much more involved' in the '88 Conference than in previous Conferences. Undoubtedly, the impressions of those taking part in the Conference were almost universally positive and warm — surpriz-ingly so.

As always of course the Conference had attempted too much. Bishop Graham Leonard (and he was not alone in this) had hoped that the Conference would tackle one main issue in detail, so that the mind of the Conference could have grown and developed in respect of this issue. Yet he along with almost all the bishops gave prime place of importance to the periods of Bible study in small groups. It was the Bible study groups which were the building blocks of this Conference. Instead of holding these in a plenary session, the participants met in small groups which stayed together throughout the Conference not only for the study of Bishop John Taylor's remarkable Bible Studies, *Briefing the Apostles*, but also for the sections.

The groups were very mixed: one included Bishop Graham Leonard together with Bishop Browning, Margaret Hewitt (notably against women's ordination) and the Revd Nan Peete (presumably notably for women's ordination). 'Much of our time', commented one group, is spent

> 'in small groups of about ten bishops. Each day we study the Bible together, pray and talk at length about a particular subject — in our case the place of the laity in the mission and ministry of the Church. Like other groups we come from sharply contrasted backgrounds and cultures, and with a variety of theological outlooks. Because of language differences, we need the help of interpreters who translate what we say into Spanish, Portugese and English.'

In that letter to the newspapers, ten of the bishops echoed what nearly all the bishops experienced throughout the three weeks of daily Bible study:

> 'This diversity, far from dividing us from each other is mutually enriching. We have grown together in love and respect for one another, discovering, in our deepening bonds of friendship and common concern for the Church's mission, the essence of what it means to be a member of the Anglican Communion.'

Along with the daily worship, such was the soil in which the fragile and elusive plant of Anglicanism grew and actually flourished in the three weeks of Lambeth '88. 'The real work of Lambeth', wrote the editor of the Lambeth Daily,

> 'is not done on paper but in the sharing of experience. No one can record the difference it has made in the lives of all participants to share worship, Bible study, conversation, food and drink and hard work with Anglicans they would never meet in any other way.'

Archbishop Andrew Mya Han of Burma was pleased that everybody had had a chance to contribute and that discussions were not dominated, as some had feared at the outset, by bishops from America or the UK. Bishop David Evans of Peru and Bolivia endorsed this favourable appraisal. Speaking of the Bible study groups he commented that they were 'one of the best features of the Conference, because of the close integration of biblical material and many of the more polemical issues' during the three weeks. 'So many of the problems are cultural clashes [which are found] in microcosm in most of the groups.' Clearly cultures became faces and people and names, and the Bible study groups as well as the section groups soon became the best arena for debate because the debate was not just abstract. 'You have to be more open to people with whom you disagree when you have been studying the Bible together.'

For the Revd Nan Peete, worship and Bible study were the foundation of Lambeth '88. 'If we don't have that we could lose the spirit and reason for being together.' For, contrary to what some press reports inferred, numbers at the daily eucharist increased, necessitating larger numbers of ministers to give communion than had at first been organized. 'We underestimated you!' exclaimed the Chaplain to the Conference, Bishop Alastair Haggart, on the fourth day: 'Very happily numbers attending the morning eucharists have exceeded our expectations.'

The Unity of Word and Worship: Scripture and Sacrament

Perhaps it will be in that distinctive duet of Word and Sacrament which so characterized Anglican protest at the Reformation, that we shall discover much of what is distinctively Anglican. For many, Archbishop Michael Ramsey, whose funeral had been held in Canterbury Cathedral three months before the Conference, embodied that distinctively Anglican spirituality which focused the Gospel and the sacramental expression of Christian life in a lay spirituality which was both pastoral and prophetic and also profoundly incarnational. The title of his first book published as long ago as 1936 gave the clue: *The Gospel and the Catholic Church*, a Church and a spirituality continually formed and reformed by the thrust and dialectic of scripture.

We experienced this in a wonderfully powerful way in the worship of Lambeth '88. We experienced it the evening that Archbishop Desmond Tutu led the Conference in prayer, fasting and vigil. He was so in line with Anglican tradition when he moved straight from scripture to spirituality: straight from the doctrine of God to the issues of social justice and peace. For Archbishop Desmond Tutu it is clearly all a seamless garment in which the Body of Christ is clothed. Bishop Jenkins put his finger on it when he was asked what united Anglicans: 'Liturgical experience in and through common prayer with a refusal to be dominated by any one theological agenda', he claimed. It was not insignificant that the Conference called for the setting up of a liturgical commission to help in weaving the texture of prayer book revisions across the worldwide Communion. For scripture, sacrament, spirituality and service all belong together. Put another way, what we believe and the way we pray are necessarily totally interrelated. Anglicanism is distinctive at this point, tracing its insistence upon a scriptural, sacramental, incarnational and lay spirituality back through Ramsey, Stephen Bayne, Temple, Gore of Mirfield (not a little responsible for the spiritual formation of Archbishop Tutu), to Bishop Andrewes (upon whom Bayne consciously modelled his prayer life), Bishop Ken, George Herbert, John Donne, Dean Colet (at the Reformation), Anselm (so beloved by Michael Ramsey). Perhaps these are only stepping stones in Anglican tradition, which does not make for streamlined travel, but they have usually proved to be sufficient for those with a truly pilgrim spirit. So do not underestimate Lambeth Conferences as instruments of unity and as structures of grace. 'I found it a very moving experience', confessed Bishop Jenkins, 'it will change nearly all of us in the jobs we are doing.' You cannot ask much more than that from a conference.

So, the question was 'When?' rather than 'Whether?' there would be another Lambeth Conference. In five years? 'Heaven forbid!' exploded Archbishop Khotso Makhulu at a press conference on the last evening. Yet that was more mischievous than meaningful because there can be little doubt that something along the lines of a Lambeth Conference is needed at regular intervals in the life of the Communion and will continue to be needed for the foreseeable future. But where such Conferences should take place is perhaps inevitably the next question.

The Archbishopric of Canterbury and the Church of England

'Bermuda?' suggested the playful Owen Chadwick after his scholarly and witty presentation to the Conference during the first week. Yet in his lecture on the history of Lambeth Conferences he had struck a serious note.

> 'Probably the most important physical symbol of this feeling for historical continuity, even an apostolic continuity, has been for these Conferences the chair of St Augustine at Canterbury. It serves as a sort of sacrament within the tradition, not unlike the purpose which the shrine of St Peter serves when people go on pilgrimage to Rome; a visible sign of an apostolic continuity . . . St Augustine was here; and so was Cranmer. It is the seed-plot of our faith and of our way of worshipping God.'

But he ventured even further:

> 'I personally think it will make for a difficulty if some future assembly decides that it would be more convenient to meet in Montreal or in Nairobi or in Bangalore . . . it is the touching of the old roots which was very important to the Canadians and Americans 121 years ago and which has been important to many of the bishops at all the Conferences since.'

It has been the African bishops both at Lambeth '78 and Lambeth '88 who have strongly opposed moving the Conference away from England for precisely these reasons. Bishop Akinbola and Bishop Akintayo, both of Nigeria, expressed the importance of the historical and apostolic continuity of 'leaving our rural dioceses, our homelands, and coming to the centre of it all — Canterbury.' Notwithstanding, many of the bishops still think otherwise. Bishop Browning would prefer 'Nairobi or somewhere preferably in one of the developing countries', he claimed.

Yet there was a warm and striking unanimity by the end of the Conference about feelings of genuine affection and admiration for the present occupant of the See of Canterbury and the chair of St Augustine. For eight years, Archbishop Runcie had done his homework, legging round the far-flung corners of the Anglican Communion and learning at first-hand what can only be learned at first-hand. The experience of those eight years marked him out and formed him in office, uniquely preparing him to take the chair at Lambeth '88.

171

The Conference clearly had no doubts about the ability or credibility of Robert Runcie as the 102nd Archbishop of Canterbury and as President of Lambeth '88. From the outset, the Conference visibly warmed to his leadership — and not least to his humour. After his first major and indeed masterly presentation, 'The Unity We Seek', the whole Conference sprang to its feet to give him an extended, standing ovation. The speech represented something of a landmark in developing a realization of Anglican identity, and was the fruit of long labours into the night hours. It had a note of challenge and was a realistic call to face the problem. Here was neither the headmaster's touch of Fisher, nor the evangelistic touch of Coggan, but rather something of the self-effacing overview of one who in his present office feels deeply called to serve the interests and unity of the worldwide Communion. It was as though he responded to the warmth and affection shown to him outside the Church of England and the English press, in contrast to the record of constant 'murmerings' at home throughout his years as Archbishop.

Bishops from overseas were shocked by the attitude of the press and the media to the Church of England in general and to the Archbishop of Canterbury in particular. Indeed at one point during the Conference, the Lambeth Communications Team turned the tables on the press, inviting the reporters to a press conference at which they (the bishops) interviewed, while the press sat on the platform to answer questions. In a lighter and more humourous vein, the following warning quietly appeared on the press-room blackboard:

'Danger! English Secular Journalists at Large!
Please do not feed the animals.'

Then, in an open letter, the Bishop of Southwark on behalf of the Lambeth Conference Communications Team rounded on Dr Edward Norman for his inaccurate and ill-informed article on the Conference in the *Sunday Telegraph*, pleading that Dr Norman (and by implication the press generally) should attempt to 'write what is actually happening here rather than that which his imagination concocts from a distance.'

Yet it ill befits the Church of England to complain about an unfair press. We need to move from a position of defensiveness to modest aggression: from maintenance to mission. Anglicanism in general and the Church of England in particular does not need to apologize for itself. Its record, which is by no means as good as it might be, is nevertheless not half as bad as it could be, or indeed as it so often appears to be. It agonizes where there is agony in our world. It refuses to give smooth answers to rough and tough questions. Anglicanism has not an undistinguished record in seeking to care for the needy and also in seeking to remove or change the structures which vitiate those needs. The Church of England's contribution, through debates in the House of Lords and from some of its bishops in public life to difficult issues such as homosexuality, education and AIDS, have been amongst some of the finest. Yet the Church of England needs to move from apology and pastoral first aid to proclamation, and from paranoia to *metanoia*. It is perhaps more likely that this will happen in an environment of hostility than in the cosy corridors of Establishment affability. It was bishops from countries of tyranny and persecution who brought to the Lambeth Conference a new confidence in the power of the Gospel. They did not expect a favourable press — far from it! Why should the Church of England?

Today we suffer from the press (if we suffer at all) through overexposure. The Archbishop of Canterbury at the end of Lambeth '88 recognized this fact and paid tribute to the generous space afforded by the press to the Conference.

Without in any way seeking to upgrade the office of Archbishop of Canterbury into anything resembling an Anglican pope, there can be no doubt that the office has evolved in the 121 years since the first Lambeth Conference. Increasingly it gives to the worldwide Communion a focus, and a sign of that Communion. After all, the Anglican Communion is still best defined as all those Churches which are in communion with the See of Canterbury. The choice of a worldwide bishop to 'head the Anglican Communion' was precisely *not* the brief given by Lambeth '88, even if such a brief were to strengthen the role which future Archbishops of Canterbury could play as instruments of unity. The premature suggestions in the press sweepstakes for Dr Runcie's successor ranged from Archbishop Eames to Khotso Makhulu. It is not their competence, however, which is in question — as indeed Dr Runcie himself endorsed. Such an appointment would be the wrong kind of animal, suggesting an order over and above the College of Bishops rather than a *primus inter pares*, who has no qualification other than the fact that as an English bishop he was selected to be Primate of all England and Archbishop of Canterbury.

Primates and Personalities

So now, what of the Primates? 'People say that the animal is tall, covered completely with hair, and can run quickly and laugh.' On 3rd August, during Lambeth '88, *The Guardian* newspaper reported another kind of primate, quoting Reuter's in Beijing, which was 'not a human, a bear or an ape'. So we need to distinguish carefully. The College of Primates — the other sort — has discovered a new identity in Anglicanism in recent years. Each self-governing Church in the Communion has its prime bishop and it is in this body of Primates that the mind of the Conference has been focused in recent years. They held a conspicuous position at Lambeth '88, collectively and individually. Archbishop Eames of Armagh brought articulate scholarship to Lambeth and also real qualities of leadership from the Church of Ireland, set as it is in the midst of terrorism and murder.

Archbishop Desmond Tutu, also from a Church located in struggle and suffering, was, of course, inevitably, the star of the Conference. It would be unfair to say that he dominated the Conference, for nothing could be further from his character than the wish to dominate. However, he is more of a world figure than any other bishop or archbishop and not only in the Anglican Communion but possibly in all the Churches.

Archbishop Michael Peers, both in his speeches to the plenary sessions and also in the chair, emerged as a strong leader within the Communion. A linguist, coming from a Church which is increasingly French-speaking, he insisted on chairing the Conference in French. Somehow when a vote is called for in French, it seems more courtly and less aggressive: *Ceux qui sont pour? Contre?* — French is indeed the language of diplomacy. Both Primates from the North American continent gave articulate leadership at Lambeth '88. Bishop Edmond Browning, the Presiding Bishop of ECUSA, did not overplay his hand at the Conference, but kept rather a low profile. Nevertheless, when he spoke he was to the point, clear and firm.

It fell to the Archbishop of the Indian Ocean, French Chang-Him, to chair a difficult day with many and difficult resolutions. His bilingual style was gently firm, very much the iron hand in the French-speaking velvet glove. Perhaps one of the most impressive figures at the Conference both in speech and presence was the President Bishop of the Episcopal Church in Jerusalem and the Middle East, Bishop

Samir Kafity. As Bishop of Jerusalem and a third generation Anglican, he spoke with passion of the place of Anglicanism in the world, and in particular of its important and distinctive role in the Middle East, referring to himself as the 'barbed wire bishop'.

These are just some of the Primates upon whom will devolve so much of the on-going responsibility for continuing and for implementing the resolutions and concerns of Lambeth '88. 'For swift and effective action, whether on doctrinal questions or for concentrated support in time of crisis, you need easy communication', Archbishop Runcie reminded the Conference, leaving it in no doubt as to whom both he and they should look to for such support and action: namely those 'hairy,' 'humourous' and swiftly moving Primates.

The Priority of Evangelism

The priority of evangelism was clearly underlined on the signposts leaving Canterbury at the end of Lambeth '88. The bishops left the Conference with a renewed mandate spelling out their responsibilities as apostles in an apostolic Church. Bishop Alden Hathaway of Pittsburgh wrote a passionate letter to the *Lambeth Daily* urging the priority of evangelism in the lengthy agenda of Lambeth. Bishop Browning endorsed this priority in an interview, when he said that at least the Episcopal Church in America was now beginning to 'recapture the conviction that evangelism is not an option' — that in reality there is not a conflict of priority between evangelism and social issues. Certainly, Anglicanism at its best has held these two priorities together in a single commitment to mission. Hence Bishop Luiz Prado was right on-target when he spoke with some passion of the mission in that part of the Church for which he is responsible in South Brazil:

> 'For me, being a priest and a Christian means living and sharing with the people their experiences and struggles. . . . Our vocation and our commitment is to defend and to fight for life which is God's greatest gift.'

And the mandate for all of this? 'Both the Old Testament and the Gospels are about the problems of poor rural communities often forced to be nomads. This resembles the experience of our parishioners', the bishop concluded, 'and they understand that.'

175

Last Words and Last Laughs

At the closing service in Canterbury Cathedral it was left to Bishop Browning to make a strong appeal for unity and for staying together even while disagreeing on many points of doctrine and church practice. In telling words, he reminded his fellow bishops as they prepared to make the long journey back to their dispersed dioceses:

> 'We must make the sacrifices required for our common fellowship, the common ministry, and the common service to the world which are the marks of the Catholic Church. We must be obedient to our given unity in Christ ... The Anglican Communion must empty itself, and abandon not its diversities, but our separateness. To have unity, to have authority, the Anglican Communion must not be a museum of the past, but the household of faith for the future.'

One newspaper commented that by the time Sunday, 7th August, dawned, and not least as Archbishop Runcie took his farewell of the bishops and their wives, he 'seemed about five, perhaps even ten years younger at the end of it all than at the beginning.' (He is in fact just 67.) Yet, even up to and including his last speech, Archbishop Runcie maintained a note of humour in all Conference deliberations.

> 'The first Lambeth Conference lasted four days; the second, in 1878, lasted four weeks. If succeeding Lambeth Conferences had lengthened at the same rate they would now last over ten years, and there would be no need for us to go home at all.'

But as Bishop Frank Cerveny joked towards the end of the Conference:

> 'Intimacy can only go so far and three weeks is quite far enough!'

No, in the words of T.S. Eliot, we would do better to admit to that:

> 'The brain allows one half-formed thought to pass:
> "Well, now that's done: And I'm glad it's over." '

Appendix ❋

EXTRACTS FROM THE DRAFT PASTORAL LETTERS OF
LAMBETH '88 FOR REFLECTION AND DISCUSSION

MISSION AND MINISTRY

'Personal evangelism, nurturing disciples, practical caring and the struggle for justice are bound up together and belong together. . . . Different ones among us may be more gifted or concerned for the one or the other, but we all need each other. None must deprecate the others' ministry.'

'We have to break out of being a mere club for our own members, to break the purely pastoral model to become a movement in mission.'

'Growth in prayer and response to careful preaching and teaching must lead Church members to engage in evangelism and service.'

'We urge each baptized member of our communion to take responsibility for working with the clergy in ministering the love of God, and to do so within the local congregation and within the local community.'

QUESTIONS
1) How can Anglicans help each other to share their faith in Jesus Christ with others who do not come to church? What part should the clergy play in this process?
2) If all are baptized for ministry, what are the various ministries which are necessary for building up the body of Christ?
3) Where and how do mission and ministry begin for me in my church and neighbourhood?

ECUMENICAL RELATIONS

'Our work for Christian unity is linked to our quest for human unity.'

'Prayer is the most important of all ecumenical activity. Prayer changes hearts, and it is our hearts most of all that need to be changed. "We shall only pass through the door of ecumenism on our knees".' (Yves Congar)

QUESTIONS
1) In what ways can 'unity' become exclusive and divisive in the life of the Churches and in the life of the world?

2) In what practical ways can we express our unity with other Christians at the local level? What is the relation between healing and unity?

CHRISTIANITY AND THE SOCIAL ORDER

'Whatever our understanding and interpretation of family, it remains the essential building block in the living structure of Church and society; it remains, in various forms, the fundamental institution of human community.'

'Jesus also rescues the family from being idolized. He pits it against higher, "Kingdom" commitments.' 'The Church must continually review and refine its pastoral ministries in situations of divorce, homosexuality, and any sexual relationship outside marriage.'

'Raising the status of women is an important part of caring for God's world.'

'Where governments are doing God's will by working for the welfare of all their people in the fight against the giants of poverty, ignorance and disease, they should be supported by the Churches. But they should also be subject to constructive criticism as all of us are under judgement.'

QUESTIONS

1) What forces today are making for the fragmentation of family life? In what practical ways can we counter these forces? What other 'higher commitments' rightly displace family commitments? In what ways has the disease AIDS made it more difficult for the Church to teach chastity?
3) In what practical ways can the Christian community help to make government more caring for the poor, the homeless and the marginalized in our society?

DOGMATIC AND PASTORAL CONCERNS

'It is through Christ that God wills to be with others and to receive them with love and mercy, just as He has received us. Christ is the one who holds the door open.'

'To everyone of his followers, Jesus' question is the same one he puts to his disciples. (Mark 8:29) "Who do you say that I am?" '

'We affirm that the scriptures are best seen as the Church's books.... Through the ages, the living and growing 'mind' of the Church has best been formed when the Church has been attentive to listening to and receiving the scriptural word within the fullest life of its liturgy, teaching, prayer and Christian community.'

QUESTIONS

1) In what ways is the Gospel changing and yet unchangeable?
2) Daily Bible reading is part of the Anglican recitation of the daily office. In what other ways can clergy and laity receive the scriptures, individually and corporately?